Biography Today

*Profiles
of People
of Interest
to Young
Readers*

Volume 17
Issue 1
January 2008

Cherie D. Abbey
Managing Editor

Omnigraphics

P.O. Box 31-
Detroit, MI 482

D1417099

Cherie D. Abbey, *Managing Editor*

Peggy Daniels, Joan Goldsworthy, Jeff Hill, Laurie Hillstrom,
Eve Nagler, and Diane Telgen, *Sketch Writers*

Allison A. Beckett and Mary Butler, *Research Staff*

* * *

Peter E. Ruffner, *Publisher*
Matthew P. Barbour, *Senior Vice President*

* * *

Elizabeth Collins, *Research and Permissions Coordinator*
Kevin M. Hayes, *Operations Manager*
Cherry Stockdale, *Permissions Assistant*

Shirley Amore, Martha Johns, and Kirk Kauffman, *Administrative Staff*

The information in this publication was compiled from the sources cited and from other sources considered reliable. While every possible effort has been made to ensure reliability, the publisher will not assume liability for damages caused by inaccuracies in the data, and makes no warranty, express or implied, on the accuracy of the information contained herein.

This book is printed on acid-free paper meeting the ANSI Z39.48 Standard. The infinity symbol that appears above indicates that the paper in this book meets that standard.

Printed in the United States

INDEXED IN
Children's Magazine Guide

Contents

Preface

Biography Today is a magazine designed and written for the young reader—ages 9 and above—and covers individuals that librarians and teachers tell us that young people want to know about most: entertainers, athletes, writers, illustrators, cartoonists, and political leaders.

The Plan of the Work

The publication was especially created to appeal to young readers in a format they can enjoy reading and readily understand. Each issue contains approximately 10 sketches arranged alphabetically. Each entry provides at least one picture of the individual profiled, and bold-faced rubrics lead the reader to information on birth, youth, early memories, education, first jobs, marriage and family, career highlights, memorable experiences, hobbies, and honors and awards. Each of the entries ends with a list of easily accessible sources designed to lead the student to further reading on the individual and a current address. Retrospective entries are also included, written to provide a perspective on the individual's entire career.

Biographies are prepared by Omnigraphics editors after extensive research, utilizing the most current materials available. Those sources that are generally available to students appear in the list of further reading at the end of the sketch.

Indexes

Cumulative indexes are an important component of *Biography Today*. Each issue of the *Biography Today* General Series includes a Cumulative Names Index, which comprises all individuals profiled in *Biography Today* since the series began in 1992. In addition, we compile three other indexes: the Cumulative General Index, Places of Birth Index, and Birthday Index. See our web site, www.biographytoday.com, for these three indexes, along with the Names Index. All *Biography Today* indexes are cumulative, including all individuals profiled in both the General Series and the Subject Series.

Our Advisors

This series was reviewed by an Advisory Board comprising librarians, children's literature specialists, and reading instructors to ensure that the concept of this publication—to provide a readable and accessible biographical magazine for young readers—was on target. They evaluated the title as it developed, and their suggestions have proved invaluable. Any errors, however, are ours alone. We'd like to list the Advisory Board members, and to thank them for their efforts.

Gail Beaver
Adjunct Lecturer
University of Michigan
Ann Arbor, MI

Cindy Cares
Youth Services Librarian
Southfield Public Library
Southfield, MI

Carol A. Doll
School of Information Science and Policy
University of Albany, SUNY
Albany, NY

Kathleen Hayes-Parvin
Language Arts Teacher
Birney Middle School
Southfield, MI

Karen Imarisio
Assistant Head of Adult Services
Bloomfield Twp. Public Library
Bloomfield Hills, MI

Rosemary Orlando
Director
St. Clair Shores Public Library
St. Clair Shores, MI

Our Advisory Board stressed to us that we should not shy away from controversial or unconventional people in our profiles, and we have tried to follow their advice. The Advisory Board also mentioned that the sketches might be useful in reluctant reader and adult literacy programs, and we would value any comments librarians might have about the suitability of our magazine for those purposes.

Your Comments Are Welcome

Our goal is to be accurate and up-to-date, to give young readers information they can learn from and enjoy. Now we want to know what you think. Take a look at this issue of *Biography Today*, on approval. Write or call me with your comments. We want to provide an excellent source of biographical information for young people. Let us know how you think we're doing.

Cherie Abbey
Managing Editor, *Biography Today*
Omnigraphics, Inc.
P.O. Box 31-1640
Detroit, MI 48231-1640

editor@biographytoday.com
www.biographytoday.com

Congratulations!

Congratulations to the following individuals and libraries who are receiving a free copy of *Biography Today*, Vol. 17, No. 1, for suggesting people who appear in this issue.

Mollie Ballard, Vienna Elementary School, Vienna, WV

Paul Bishette, Silan Bronson Library, Waterbury, CT

Paige Hisiro, Harrisburg, PA

Lennie Hurst, GCI Intermediate School, Paragould, AR

Uzmah Khan, Independence K-8-Elkhorn, Lodi, CA

Noel Miranda, Harmon Johnson Elementary School, Sacramento, CA

Carolyn Torre, William L. Buck School Library, Valley Stream, NY

Miranda Trimm, L.E. White Middle School, Allegan, MI

Greta Binford 1965-
American Biologist and Arachnologist
Pioneering Researcher in Spider Venom

BIRTH

Greta Binford was born on September 17, 1965, in Craw-fordsville, Indiana, a small city some 40 miles northwest of the state capital of Indianapolis. She was the second child of David and Pamela (Crull) Binford. Her parents owned a small farm where they grew corn and soybeans and raised cattle; Pamela Binford also taught elementary school. Binford's older brother, Greg, became an academic researcher, studying soil chemistry as a professor of agronomy at the University of Delaware.

YOUTH

Growing up on a rural farm, Binford lived the life of a "classic tomboy," she recalled. She had hours of unsupervised play time that she often spent by a creek, catching minnows and crawfish. When her father said she could keep a stray cat and its litter of kittens if she fed them herself, "I made a fishing pole and caught chubs to feed the cats." Spending so much time outside, she developed a curiosity about the natural world—including spiders, which were just one of many creatures that she observed. One time, she remembered, "my friend Sheila and I spent hours in search of the 'ancient lost mastodon' and wandered around poking at large piles of cow manure looking for evidence. I guess it's safe to say that I've never been afraid of getting dirty."

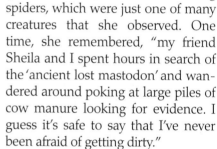

"My friend Sheila and I spent hours in search of the 'ancient lost mastodon' and wandered around poking at large piles of cow manure looking for evidence. I guess it's safe to say that I've never been afraid of getting dirty."

Binford brought energy and enthusiasm to her school activities as well. While attending high school at North Montgomery High School in Crawfordsville, Binford was a versatile athlete, participating in gymnastics, track (as a sprinter), and cheerleading for all four years. She also spent one season diving for her swim team and played trombone in her marching band as a freshman. Although she made the honor society, she confessed that "I was not a super ambitious or driven student," for she had yet to find a subject that kindled any passion. "There were times when I wanted to be a farm wife and have a huge garden, and a lot of dogs and horses," she recalled. "At another extreme, at one point in junior high I wanted to be a disk jockey. In my wildest dreams I wanted a horse ranch somewhere out west."

Biology was a favorite subject in high school, but Binford didn't know how to turn it into a career. When she entered college, she discovered that research could give her those kinds of opportunities, but "at that time the thought of being in school for a long time was not appealing." It was only later she would discover the luxury of being able "to focus and learn deeply about things that you find fundamentally interesting."

EDUCATION

Binford graduated in 1983 from North Montgomery High School and entered Purdue University. She majored in veterinary medicine until she discovered she couldn't overcome feeling "squeamish about sick animals." She then studied psychology until leaving school to get married. In 1987 she began taking classes at a branch of Miami University in Ohio with the hopes of becoming a science teacher. While taking a genetics class there, the professor invited Binford to spend a summer in the Amazon region of South America observing spiders—a summer that changed the course of her life. In 1990 she earned her Bachelor of Arts (BA) degree in zoology, cum laude (with honors), from Miami University. Three years later she received her Master of Science (MS) degree in biology from the University of Utah. In 2000 she completed her doctorate (PhD) in ecology and evolutionary biology at the University of Arizona.

CAREER HIGHLIGHTS

Discovering Diversity of Spiders

Binford's first expedition awakened an intense scientific curiosity within her. In 1988, while a student at Miami University in Ohio, she traveled with genetics professor Ann Rypstra to the Amazon jungles of Peru. There, she helped Rypstra study an unusual type of spider that created and shared giant webs. Rypstra hoped the observations would help them understand how social behavior developed. She set Binford to observe these social spiders, *Anelosimus eximius,* for hours every morning. The student would sit next to a web—some of them were as large as a semi-trailer-and take notes. "Most of what I'd heard about spiders was nasty, evil stuff—and all I saw was really beautiful," she remembered. The species she studied worked together to build webs, capture large prey such as locusts or even tarantulas, and care for each other's offspring.

When Binford returned home to Ohio she immediately changed her major to zoology. "It was a combination of the biology of that species being cool, and being surrounded by all of the Amazonian diversity that piqued my desire to learn all I could about biodiversity," she recalled. "The realization that I could actually make a contribution to our understanding of the biology of these animals really inspired me." She got divorced around this time, leaving her free to continue her education and perform research wherever she chose.

As Binford studied more about spiders, she discovered diversity in how they capture prey. Spiders can build webs in trees, on the ground, or even in water; others don't build webs, but use silk as weapons or lures; some spiders lie in wait to trap prey, while others attack prey by jumping or spitting. Almost all of the 40,000 known species of spiders, also known as arachnids, have venom. Spider venoms can be very complex, made up of as many as 200 different chemical compounds. While doing research for her doctorate, Binford studied spiders' methods for capturing prey. She became "curious about how venom composition might change as feeding behaviors change," for in studying venom, "the species-level diversity is magnified in the chemical diversity of the venoms."

"There aren't any spiders for which we know all the chemicals in their venom—none," Binford explained.

Unfortunately, little research had been done on spider venoms. "There aren't any spiders for which we know all the chemicals in their venom—none," Binford explained. After earning her doctorate, she began studying the venom of the brown recluse spider, because "we knew something about the venoms because of their medical effects on humans. This gave me a starting place for studying how the venoms vary among species in the group, and a way to study the venom diversity and evolution." Binford spent over two years in postdoctoral research with Dr. Michael Wells of the Department of Biochemistry and Molecular Biophysics at the University of Arizona, learning to analyze spider venoms of the brown recluse and its relatives, the genus *Loxosceles.*

Because most spider venom targets insects, humans—whose anatomy is completely different—aren't usually affected by spider bites. "If we were wired for spider venoms the way insects are, we'd be screwed," Binford noted. In the United States, only two kinds of spiders produce venom proven to be dangerous to people: the brown recluse and the black widow (genus *Latrodectus)*. Black widow venom contains neurotoxins, chemicals that affect nerves and muscles and can cause cramps, spasms, fever, and even death. A cure for black widow venom, known as an *antivenin* or *antivenom,* has been available for decades, and very few people die from black widow bites anymore.

The brown recluse spider and other *Loxosceles* spiders are also known as "fiddleback" spiders because of the violin-shaped marking on their head and thorax. (This marking can be very faint in some species, so the spider's distinctive pattern of three pairs of eyes, rather than the more common four pairs, is a better identifier.) *Loxosceles* spiders produce a different kind of poison than black widows, called a cytotoxin. It kills cells surrounding

SCIENTIFIC CLASSIFICATION

Scientific classification, also called taxonomy, is a method of organizing the millions of earth's living organisms into similar groups. Swedish botanist Carolus Linnaeus was the first to propose this system, in his 1735 text Systema Naturae. His work developed into the modern system scientists use to name and catalog everything from bacteria to primates. While biologists sometimes debate the best way to group and place organisms, they all find taxonomy a useful tool for comparing and discussing different creatures.

The largest groupings are called kingdoms. Most commonly, scientists divide life into five different kingdoms: animals, plants, fungi, monera (bacteria and other organisms with simple cells), and protista (protozoa and certain algaes). Kingdoms are divided into phyla (plural for phylum), which in turn are divided into classes, then orders, then families. Finally, an organism is classified into a genus and species, which give it its two-word scientific name. Two creatures are considered members of the same species if a mating would produce fertile offspring.

Scientific names are taken from Latin, to keep them standard throughout the world. They are always italicized; genus names are capitalized and can be abbreviated to a single initial. Homo sapiens is the scientific name for humans; Loxosceles reclusa is the scientific name for the brown recluse spiders. This is how both species would be classified scientifically:

	Human	Brown recluse spider
Kingdom	Animalia	Animalia
Phylum	Chordata (vertebrates and close relatives)	Arthropods (insects, arachnids, crustaceans)
Class	Mammalia (mammals)	Arachnida (8-legged arthropods)
Order	Primata (primates)	Araneae (spiders)
Family	Hominids (upright posture and large brains)	Sicariidae (spiders with cytotoxic poison)
Genus	Homo	Loxosceles
Species	H. sapiens	L. reclusa

the bite area, leaving open wounds that can take weeks to heal. In very rare instances, the venom can affect a person's red blood cells, causing them to burst (a condition called *hemolysis*). *Loxosceles* bites are very rarely fatal; in fact, other conditions are often mistaken for recluse spider bites, including bacterial infections, Lyme disease and other tick-borne illnesses, herpes simplex virus, and other insect or spider bites. In 2001, an infant with anthrax contracted from the attack on NBC News headquarters in New York was misdiagnosed with a brown recluse bite.

——— " ———

Recluse spiders fascinate Binford because of the unique way their venom affects people. When it ruptures cells, "the problem that causes the damage in people is an immune reaction . . . a complex cascade of immune events that we're still trying to fully understand."

——— " ———

Recluse spiders fascinate Binford because of the unique way their venom affects people. When it ruptures cells, "the problem that causes the damage in people is an immune reaction . . . a complex cascade of immune events that we're still trying to fully understand," she explained. There are around 80 different species of *Loxosceles* in the Americas and over 100 worldwide, including some in Africa, the Caribbean, the Mediterranean, and China. She has traveled as far as Costa Rica, Peru, Argentina, South Africa, and Namibia (in southwest Africa) in search of various recluse specimens. She has also found a transplanted South American relative of the brown recluse, a species called *Loxosceles laeta*, in a Los Angeles Goodwill store. For Binford, field work is "like a scavenger hunt," she explained. "We study old published papers and museum records for locality information, and piece together an itinerary that will take us to as many species in the group as possible." By collecting spiders (including live specimens) and taking them back to her laboratory, she can collect, analyze, and compare different species.

Sharing Her Enthusiasm for Science

Since 2003 Binford has been an assistant professor of biology at Lewis & Clark College in Portland, Oregon. In her lab there, she has a collection of over 600 spiders, both of *Loxosceles* and their closest relatives, the genus *Sicarius*. (This genus includes the six-eyed crab spider and similar desert spiders of Africa and South America.) To figure out how these species are related, Binford and the students under her supervision perform various

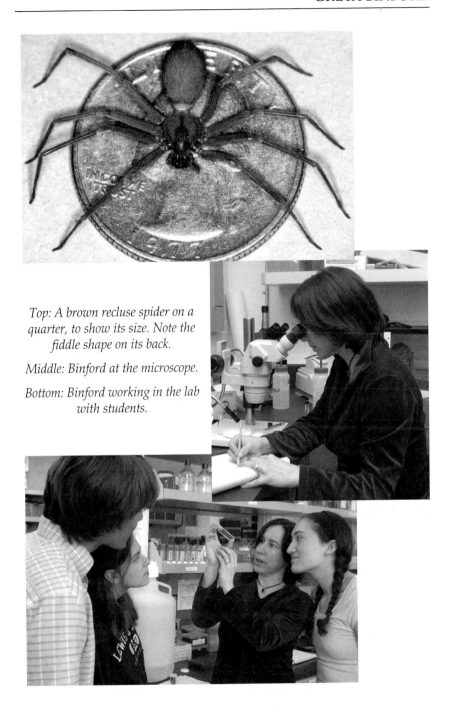

Top: *A brown recluse spider on a quarter, to show its size. Note the fiddle shape on its back.*

Middle: *Binford at the microscope.*

Bottom: *Binford working in the lab with students.*

analyses. They study feeding and mating behavior; they also study the morphology (color and shape) of the spiders to see if they belong to a known species. "Students learn to do basic work that is involved in identifying and describing new species," she related. "So far we have found at least four new species."

Binford's lab also performs more sophisticated studies of the spiders. They get DNA samples by removing legs from spiders (this does no lasting harm to the spiders, and many lab specimens can live as long as five or six years). Using modern techniques of molecular biology, including gene sequencing, they can isolate and reproduce specific genes. "We then analyze these gene sequences using something called phylogenetic analysis and come up with a 'family tree' of species relationships for this group," she explained. Computer programs are an important part of this work as well.

——— *"* ———

"I will grab spiders in my hands, but only if I have no other option and I know that the species is harmless. My students and I always capture and transport our toxic spiders by putting them in collecting vials, which does not require physically touching the spider."

——— *"* ———

Besides studying the biology and genetics of Sicariidae spiders, Binford and her students analyze their subjects' venom as well. She collects venom from her spiders in a process known as "milking" the spider. It's a tricky technique, because most *Loxosceles* bodies are only about the size of a toothpaste cap. First, she puts the spiders to sleep with carbon dioxide gas. Using tweezers to handle the spider, she examines it under a microscope and washes its fangs. She gives the spider a small electrical shock to contract its venom glands. She has to be careful when collecting the venom, because the shock also makes the spider vomit and she has to keep the two fluids from mixing.

With pure samples of venom, Binford and her team can test how they work by injecting them into live crickets. "We also isolate and sequence genes that are being expressed in the venoms, which is a way to see what toxins spiders are making and using for prey immobilization," she explained. "For each of these pieces of information we map it on the tree of species and analyze patterns of diversity. This tells us a lot about how the venoms have evolved." Binford encourages her students to participate in all of her research, from the simplest observations to the more complex genetic analyses.

Searching for six-eyed sand spiders in small outcrop caves in Namibia. Binford is to the right; an undergradate student is in the center; and colleague Pablo Barea Nunez is on the left.

The National Science Foundation has recognized Binford for involving her students in her research. In 2006 they awarded her a five-year CAREER grant worth over $600,000 to help fund her work. "It's an integrative project," she explained, "meaning I do research that's both working with the animals themselves . . . and I'm also doing molecular biology focusing on the toxin." By involving her students in all stages of this research, they learn about the scientific process as well as "a lot about the biodiversity of the spider group." Through these efforts, students can learn "what science is and just how careful you have to be to learn something with confidence," Binford said. "I hope that, fundamentally, my students learn to be creative and critical thinkers, and that if they want to, they too can contribute to our understanding of the natural world." She hopes they will also learn that "we are surrounded by, and dependent upon, a vast diversity of living organisms about which we have much left to learn."

Searching for Practical Research Applications

One of the benefits of performing research into biodiversity is the potential for beneficial practical applications, like medical treatments. As part of her research, Binford has learned more about a specific chemical toxin in *Lox-*

17

osceles and *Sicarius* venom called sphingomyelinase D (SMD). Working with Matt Cordes, an assistant professor in biochemistry at the University of Arizona, she discovered that SMD is shared with a strain of bacteria, *Corynebacteria,* that infects farm animals. It is a rare instance where genes have been transferred between two completely different species—something especially rare between bacteria and more complex organisms. Binford can't yet prove which species gave the toxin to the other, but suspects the spider is the more likely donor. This discovery is another piece of the puzzle of biological diversity, and may help in developing treatments for both recluse bites and corynebacterial infections.

———— " ————

"I really liked the spitting spiders and jumping spiders in **Eight Legged Freaks.** *Those are some of my favorite spiders in general and even though they were horrifyingly large in that movie, I liked the fact that they were based on the biological reality of what those spiders do at a microscale."*

———— " ————

Already, a Mexican company called Bioclon has used Binford's research to create an antivenom for *Loxosceles* bites. (It is not yet available in the U.S.) In testing, it reduces the pain of the bite and allows lesions to begin healing within a day. Binford hopes that by understanding more about the composition and effects of spider venom, "we will be able to create diagnostics and treatments that will not just work on one species but will work across the entire breadth of species with this toxin, and that includes some pretty unrelated animals." The scientist added: "If you're camping in Peru and you're bitten by something and you have a little antivenom in your pocket, will it work? It's fundamentally an evolutionary question."

In all her years of studying arachnids, however, Binford has only been bitten once: by a social spider during her undergraduate days. "I deserved it (inadvertently smashed it against its cage) and barely felt it," she recalled. Since then she has handled tens of thousands of spiders without incident. Of course, "handling rarely means actually touching them with my hands," she explained. "I will grab spiders in my hands, but only if I have no other option and I know that the species is harmless. My students and I always capture and transport our toxic spiders by putting them in collecting vials, which does not require physically touching the spider." But peo-

Collecting spiders in Argentina.
Binford is on the left, and an undergraduate student is on the right.

ple shouldn't be afraid of spiders, she added: "They will only bite if they're in danger of being crushed or in danger themselves. Mostly, they just want to run away and find bugs." Besides, "without spiders there would be a lot more insects and a lot fewer plants." If people would just take the time to watch, she said, spiders "are going about their lives doing very interesting things in your own back yard. Stepping outside and simply watching them can be immensely rewarding."

Unfortunately, popular culture doesn't provide many positive images of spiders. "Outside of *Charlotte's Web,* spiders are nearly universally depicted as objects of horror, evil, and doom—very much unfair," Binford said. She did her part to make spiders appealing by contributing to the 2002 film *Spider-Man.* She served as a consultant to the art department; the lab where Peter Parker is bitten by a spider is very similar to her own. She admitted that "I really liked the spitting spiders and jumping spiders in *Eight Legged Freaks.* Those are some of my favorite spiders in general and even though they were horrifyingly large in that movie, I liked the fact that they were based on the biological reality of what those spiders do at a microscale." Besides the spiders that spit toxic glue to trap prey, other spiders Binford finds fascinating are those that throw a silk string with glue at the tip to catch moths, and brightly colored jumping spiders, which stalk prey like a cat does.

For Binford, it is this variety that makes spider research so intriguing. Besides the 40,000 known species of arachnids, "we know there are at least twice as many that are still undescribed. . . . There could be tens of thousands still out there we don't know about." No one knows what kinds of treatments might be found in spider venom, although other researchers have discovered potential for heart and diabetes drugs in tarantula venoms. "What's exciting for many people about [spider venom] is that the specificity with which they target the nervous system is really impressive, and we've learned a lot from that specificity, about the diversity of what are called ion channels in the nervous system," Binford said. "And there's a lot of excitement about potential for drugs and insecticides and specific applications of that diversity."

> "
>
> *"I'm happiest in the field, flipping over rocks to see what crawls out," she said. "There's a whole world that lives under rocks and in wood. Being in touch with the natural history of the organism you study is the starting point for any good researcher."*
>
> "

In the meantime, *Loxosceles* still holds endless fascination for Binford—and endless possibilities. "There's an evolutionary puzzle here," she noted. "I'd like to know where SMD originated, how it originated, and what it's doing for the spider." In addition, "there are still big aspects of spider biology that we don't know much about." Spider family trees have been arranged by common physical characteristics (morphology), but she hopes DNA sequencing can provide more definitive answers about the relationship between various species. So she will continue searching for spiders to examine and classify. "I'm happiest in the field, flipping over rocks to see what crawls out," she said. "There's a whole world that lives under rocks and in wood. Being in touch with the natural history of the organism you study is the starting point for any good researcher." Her lab work is just as interesting, she remarked. "It's surprising to me how few of us study spider venom. It's just so cool."

HOME AND FAMILY

Binford was married and divorced while still in college. Currently, she lives in Portland, Oregon, with her fiancé, Dr. Keith Dede, a professor of Chinese linguistics at Lewis & Clark College. They have three pets: a 15-year-old border collie-chow mix named Zoey, and two young cats, Gourgu (Manchu for "beast") and Meme (Chinese for "little beauty").

HOBBIES AND OTHER INTERESTS

Binford enjoys dancing and listening to live music in the alternative coun-try, funk, and bluegrass genres—so much so that she is learning to play the mandolin. She also enjoys outdoor activities like hiking and camping, as well as more homebound pursuits, such as gardening and cooking with her fiancé. When she has spare time, she likes to read fiction.

HONORS AND AWARDS

CAREER Award (National Science Foundation): 2006

FURTHER READING

Periodicals

Lewis & Clark College Chronicle, Summer 2004
New Yorker, Mar. 5, 2007, p.66
Northwest Science & Technology, Fall 2006
Oregonian, July 21, 2007, p.B12
South Bend Tribune, Sep. 24, 2000, p.D7

Online Articles

http://www.orato.com/node/2429
    (Orato, "I'm Spider-Woman," May 17, 2007)

Other

Binford, Greta, e-mail interview for *Biography Today,* Aug. 2007
"The Bliss of the Spider Women," Talk of the Nation: Science Friday
    (transcript), NPR, Mar. 16, 2007

ADDRESS

Greta Binford
Department of Biology
Lewis & Clark College
0615 S.W. Palantine Hill Rd., Mailstop 53
Portland, OR 97219

WORLD WIDE WEB SITE

http://www.lclark.edu

Cory Booker 1969-
American Political Leader
Mayor of Newark, New Jersey

BIRTH

Cory Anthony Booker was born on April 27, 1969, in Washington, DC. He is the son of Cary Booker Sr. and Carolyn Booker. Both of his parents worked for IBM and were among the first African Americans to hold executive positions with the company, with his father specializing in sales and his mother working as personnel director. He has one older brother, Cary Jr.

YOUTH

Cory Booker's parents played an active role in the civil rights movement of the 1960s, and their willingness to directly confront issues of race and discrimination had a strong influence on their children. At about the time that Cory was born, Cary and Carolyn Booker chose to purchase a new home in northern New Jersey and made an offer on a house in the prosperous community of Harrington Park. At that time, the town was almost entirely populated by white residents, and some individuals wanted to prevent minorities from moving into the area. The Bookers were told that the house they wished to purchase had already been sold, but they suspected that this was a lie intended to keep them from living in the city. They sought help from the New Jersey Fair Housing Commission, which secured proof of the realtor's illegal racial discrimination, and the Bookers were soon able to buy the house.

> "They gave me everything I could dream of," Booker said about his parents, "raised me in one of the country's wealthiest suburbs, rooted me in the culture of this country, black culture. I would have betrayed all the opportunities I've had if I didn't give something back."

Cory and Cary Booker had the distinction of being the first African-American students in the local elementary school, and Cory later described his family's presence in Harrington Park as being "like four raisins in a tub of vanilla ice cream." Regardless of whatever awkwardness he may have felt, Cory soon began to impress others with his intelligence and responsible behavior. "He was always so levelheaded," his mother later observed. "Even now it amazes me." Booker has explained that, from an early age, he was encouraged by his parents to work hard in his studies and "to be part of the struggle" for social justice and civil rights. The example set by his mother and father ended up being a big reason why he later sought a career in public service. "They gave me everything I could dream of," he said, "raised me in one of the country's wealthiest suburbs, rooted me in the culture of this country, black culture. I would have betrayed all the opportunities I've had if I didn't give something back."

EDUCATION

Booker excelled as a student, and his outgoing personality made him well known to the students and staff at the schools he attended. "He was the kind of guy who slowed you down when you hung around him," said his longtime friend Chris Magarro, "because he'd say 'hi' to everyone. . . . The kids, the teachers, the janitors. Everyone." At Northern Valley Regional High School at Old Tappan, he was elected class president in his senior year. He was also an outstanding athlete, earning all-state honors in football prior to his graduation in 1987.

Booker's abilities on the gridiron earned him a football scholarship to Stanford University in Palo Alto, California, where he played tight end for the Cardinals. By the time he reached his senior year, he was being viewed as a prospective NFL player. But football was just one part of his college life. He was equally impressive as a student and volunteer, putting in long hours to master his subjects and also devoting time to tutoring young people and to working at a crisis intervention hotline in Palo Alto. As in high school, he proved himself a leader among his fellow students and was elected president of his senior class. He completed his Bachelor of Arts (BA) degree in political science with honors in 1991. He then undertook an additional year of studies at the university, earning a Master of Arts (MA) degree in sociology and urban affairs.

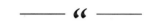

"He was the kind of guy who slowed you down when you hung around him," said his longtime friend Chris Magarro, "because he'd say 'hi' to everyone. . . . The kids, the teachers, the janitors. Everyone."

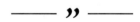

Wishing to further his education, Booker applied for one of the prestigious Rhodes Scholarships, which allow students from around the world to study at Oxford University in England. The scholarship funds two or three years of study. The program typically selects students who have demonstrated outstanding academic achievement, integrity, concern for others, and leadership ability. In 1992, Booker became one of 32 U.S. students chosen as Rhodes Scholars and spent the next two years studying modern history at the university. During his time in England, he attracted attention for becoming the president of the L'Chaim Society, a Jewish student group at Oxford, even though Booker himself is a Baptist Christian. The study of other religions has continued to be important to him, and he believes that he gains "a deeper reverence for God" by understanding how other people worship.

Booker returned to the U.S. and enrolled at Yale Law School. Upon graduating with a law degree in 1997, he possessed a very impressive education and a reputation as a charming and idealistic young leader. With his cre-

Booker played tight end at Stanford.

dentials and talents, he might have chosen any number of careers, including a high-paying position as an attorney in private practice. Instead, Booker opted to pursue community service work, and this desire led him back to his home state of New Jersey.

CAREER HIGHLIGHTS

Booker moved to the city of Newark in the mid-1990s after receiving a public interest law fellowship. He became a staff attorney for the Urban

Justice Center, where he provided legal assistance to low-income residents in housing cases, and he also worked as a program coordinator for the Newark Youth Project. In some ways, he was on familiar ground in Newark: since his childhood, he had traveled there to visit relatives, and the city is just 25 miles south of his hometown of Harrington Park.

But there is a world of difference between the affluent suburb where Booker grew up and the urban streets of Newark. Home to 273,000 people, Newark is the second-poorest city of its size in the nation, and its history over the past 50 years has not been a happy one. Once a prosperous industrial center, it faced difficulties as its factories began closing down in the decades following World War II. Unemployment and crime began to rise, and in 1967 a deadly race riot erupted in which 23 people were killed. Large numbers of residents moved out of the city in the wake of the riot, and Newark lost nearly half of its population. Though there have been signs of improvement in the decades since, the city continues to struggle with serious problems: one third of its children live in poverty; many of its citizens are unemployed; drug dealing and other crime is widespread; and its school system suffered such acute problems that it is now managed by the State of New Jersey.

> *"You meet real American heroes in these places," he explained, "people that are doing unbelievable things against the odds—not just for themselves and their families, but also for their communities and the children around."*

The difficult conditions did not discourage Booker. In fact, he believed that it was essential to confront the problems of the nation's inner cities, and he felt that his work in Newark was a continuation of the social activism that had been carried out by his parents and others during the Civil Rights movement. "It's just a different set of challenges," he explained. "We have serious urgencies in our cities, . . . and they demand the same kind of sacrifice, the same kind of dedication" as was required of activists in the past. For Booker, this effort was part of the "fight to make America real, to make the promise and the hope of this country fully evident for everyone."

Booker chose to find out about the city's challenges first hand by moving into Brick Towers, a low-income housing project in the city's Central Ward. He soon became familiar with the residents' daily woes, which included a lack of heat and hot water and the presence of drug dealers on nearby sidewalks. Booker helped bring about improvements by filing a lawsuit against the company that managed the housing project and by organizing his neighbors to lobby for better police protection. But beyond the problems, he found life in Brick Towers to be inspiring, and his life there has helped guide his mission as a politician. "You meet real American heroes in these places," he explained, "people that are doing unbelievable things against the odds—not just for themselves and their families, but also for their communities and the children around."

"I have no disrespect for Sharpe James, but he's been in office as long as I've been alive," Booker said. "After 16 years [as mayor], anything he could have done, he should have done."

Shaking Up Newark

In 1998, Booker made his entrance into politics by running for a seat on the Newark Municipal Council. His opponent was councilman George Branch, who had been in office for 16 years. Booker was able to raise a large amount of money to finance his campaign, much of it coming from school friends and others who lived outside Newark. He won the May election, and when he took office, he was 29 years old—the youngest person to ever serve on the municipal council.

Booker's victory was seen as a challenge to the politicians who had led Newark for many years, most of whom had been in office since the 1980s or earlier. The new kid at city hall wasted little time in presenting fresh ideas. He sought to change the way that the city spent taxpayers' money, and he promoted term limits for elected officials and new guidelines on campaign donations. His proposals received little support from other members of the council, however, and were not adopted.

Crime was another major concern for Councilman Booker, and he soon showed that he was prepared to go to great lengths to draw attention to the dangerous conditions that existed in some parts of the city. In August 1999, after a violent incident at a housing complex, he went on a 10-day hunger strike to protest the lack of police protection in the area. To dramatize his action, he moved into a tent outside the project. "It transformed my life," Booker said of the protest, which soon drew in a large group of supporters. "Within 24 hours people were saying, 'You're not sleeping out there alone,' and eventually there were dozens of people sleeping under this huge wedding tent. The first morning of the strike, we had a prayer circle of four people. By the end, there were enough people for us to form a circle around two buildings. Priests, rabbis, Latinos, blacks." The following year, he confronted the city's drug problem by moving into a motor home that he parked on one of the streets where dealers had been doing a booming business. He lived there for five months.

Running for Mayor

As his first term on the municipal council came to a close, Booker set his sights on higher office: he declared himself a candidate for the mayor of Newark in the 2002 election. In doing so, he was taking on the incumbent mayor, Sharpe James, a prominent African-American leader. James had had been in the mayor's office since 1986 and had never lost an election of any kind since entering public service in 1970. Considered one of the most powerful politicians in New Jersey, James kept tight control over the city's operations, and this influence helped to assure his reelection every four years. Initially, few observers thought Booker stood much chance of winning the election.

But Booker waged an energetic campaign, going door to door throughout the city and telling voters that Newark needed a new leader to address its problems. "I have no disrespect for Sharpe James, but he's been in office as long as I've been alive," Booker said. "After 16 years [as mayor], anything he could have done, he should have done." In addition, Booker was once again able to attract large campaign donations that totaled more than $3 million, and these funds helped him to finance a range of efforts to reach out to residents.

Sharpe James and his supporters soon realized they were facing a formidable challenger and began to attack Booker in numerous ways. Though both candidates are members of the Democratic Party, James described Booker as a "Republican masquerading as a Democrat." He criticized Booker's support for a voucher system to address problems in public schools as well as the support he received from some prominent Republican politicians.

Focusing on donations to Booker's campaign, Mayor James alleged that the majority of the money came from wealthy people outside the city. James suggested that if Booker were elected, these outsiders would be able to exploit the city's low-income residents. "These wealthy businessmen are investing in an opportunity to take over Newark," the mayor said. In truth, much of Booker's financial support did come from non-residents, including such well-known figures as Stephen Spielberg and Spike Lee. Booker argued that the funds he received came with no strings attached. "I'm blessed with a circle of supporters who donate but don't want anything back," he explained. "They give because they believe in me."

The label of "outsider" was also targeted at Booker himself. The James campaign criticized Booker's prosperous suburban background and noted that he had only been in the city a handful of years. They also hinted that

2006 ACADEMY AWARD® NOMINEE FOR BEST DOCUMENTARY FEATURE

Street Fight

A film by **Marshall Curry**

"Engrossing...pulls no punches."
–Jason George, *THE NEW YORK TIMES*

Sometimes elections are won and lost in the streets...

Booker's mayoral campaign against Sharpe James
was documented in the movie Street Fight.

someone educated at such places as Oxford and Yale had little in common with Newark's residents. At times, these attacks veered into the issue of race, even though both men were black. "You have to learn how to be African American," James taunted Booker at one point, "and we don't have time to train you." The mayor even went so far as to make the untrue claim that Booker was Jewish. The increasingly bitter campaign was documented by filmmaker Marshall Curry in the motion picture *Street Fight,* which was nominated for an Academy Award.

Booker was undaunted by the criticism. When Newark voters went to the polls on May 14, 2002, he felt that he was going to emerge the winner. His hopes were dashed when the votes were tallied late that night, and Sharpe James won by the slim margin of 3,494 votes.

Carrying on the Fight

Even as he conceded defeat, Booker vowed that he would be a candidate for mayor again in the 2006 election. Having given up his municipal council seat to run for mayor, he no longer had a voice in city government. Shortly after the election he formed a non-profit group, Newark Now, to aid tenant organizations and neighborhood groups in the city. "Everything we are going to do will be about making Newark a better place," he said of the group's efforts. Over the following years, he worked to strengthen his ties to the city's residents and to overcome the impression that he was an outsider. He also continued his law career, becoming a partner in the firm Booker, Rabinowitz, Trenk, Lubetkin, Tully, DiPasquale and Webster.

Another part of Booker's strategy was to seek a closer relationship with the city's trade unions and churches. Most of these influential groups had backed Sharpe James in the 2002 election, and Booker knew they would play an important part in the next contest. His efforts paid off, and by the time that his second mayoral campaign hit full stride, he had won the allegiance of many union officials and other power brokers.

City residents were expecting an exciting rematch between Booker and James in the May 2006 election, but events took a sudden turn in late March of that year, when Mayor James suddenly announced that he was no longer seeking reelection. The reason he dropped out of the race has never been fully explained, but some observers believe that he was discouraged by the increased support that Booker had gained since 2002 and by opinion polls that showed him trailing his challenger. (In 2007, James would be indicted on corruption charges due to alleged misconduct while mayor.) Another candidate, New Jersey state senator Ronald L. Rice, entered the race after James bowed out, but with less than two months to prepare a campaign and far less money than the $6 million that Booker had raised, Rice stood little chance. On May 9, 2006, Cory Booker was elected by the widest margin of victory ever tallied in a Newark mayoral election and became the chief executive of New Jersey's largest city.

> *"Everything falls on my shoulders," Booker commented shortly after taking office. "The challenge is to switch from talking about solutions to implementing solutions."*

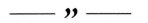

The Burden of Power

"Everything falls on my shoulders," Booker commented shortly after taking office. "The challenge is to switch from talking about solutions to implementing solutions." He soon discovered the difficulties in taking on that task. Early in his term, auditors found a $44 million shortfall in the city budget that had been created during the administration of Mayor James. As a result, Booker was forced to put through a property-tax increase to cover city expenses, which angered many homeowners. The new mayor also faced some opposition to the person he selected to be the city's new police chief, Garry McCarthy. Booker stood by his choice, however, and McCarthy was approved by the municipal council.

Bringing in a new police chief is part of Booker's focus on reducing crime, which is far and away his biggest priority. "The No. 1 issue, the No. 1 mission, the No. 1 cause for this city is to secure the safety of its citizens," he stated. "I will not stop until confidence is restored to our community." Booker has worked with Chief McCarthy and other officials to put more officers on the street, to install security cameras in the city, and to launch other safety initiatives. His anti-crime image seemed to cause concern among local gang leaders, some of whom issued death threats against Booker at the time he took office.

Many types of crime did decrease during Booker's first year in office, but the murder rate did not. A total of 106 people were killed in the city in 2006, the highest figure since 1995, with many of the murders being linked to the illegal drug trade. Statistics were similarly grim in early 2007, and then on August 4, the news got even worse. That night, four young Newark residents were confronted by a group of gunmen at a school parking lot. In what was apparently a robbery unconnected to drugs, three of the victims were forced to kneel against a wall and were shot dead at point-blank range. The fourth person was badly wounded but survived.

The seemingly random killings shocked the city and became news all across the country. Booker confronted the situation head on, overseeing the police investigation and setting up a command center in his apartment. Six suspects were arrested in the case, with one of them surrendering directly to the mayor. Booker delivered passionate eulogies at the victims' funerals and voiced his hope that the tragic incident would help galvanize the city, stating that "this is a time all Newarkers must pull together and unite around their common challenges."

The new mayor has grappled with other difficulties in 2006 and 2007, including administrative problems with a city-sponsored youth job program that left workers unpaid. In addition, a vocal group of critics mounted a recall movement to remove him from office. On the plus side, he and his staff scored some significant victories, including the removal of dozens of non-productive employees from the city payroll and the establishment of programs to help ex-convicts find jobs.

Overall, Booker is finding the mayor's job to be a challenging one. "Things come at you 1,000 miles an hour," he explained, "and much of the time you're dealing with chaos. You can easily get distracted by issues that are not central." To help maintain his focus, he frequently makes door-to-door visits throughout the city and also sets aside two days each month to discuss jobs, housing, and other concerns with residents.

Looking Ahead

Even before he became Newark's mayor, Booker was touted as a promising politician who was likely to achieve great things, and he has been recognized as one of the nation's top young leaders by such publications as *Esquire* and *Black Enterprise*. With his youth and charisma, he is often compared to former president Bill Clinton and to Illinois senator and presidential candidate Barack Obama. In fact, more than a few observers have predicted that Booker could one day become the nation's chief executive. This has led to speculation that he will seek other political office in the near future, but Booker denies this. He has said that he plans to focus on Newark for "about a decade" because he believes his work as mayor is of the utmost importance. "My loyalty, my love is here in Newark," he said, "So I'm not going anywhere."

Booker is also viewed as a new style of African-American leader who embodies the idealism of past figures but is also willing to try new approaches to difficult problems. He seems to relish this role, and he believes that the desire to serve the public is widespread among young people today. "We're sort of the hip-hop generation, we are innovators,"

he told one interviewer. "But that sense of sacrifice is still alive and well, and I see it in my neighborhoods, and I see it in the young activists I'm working with."

Booker refers often to the concept of working for a higher cause and the betterment of his city and nation, and he considers this to be an essential part of his political quest. In talking about his own efforts to become mayor, he described the struggle as a lesson of hope. "If you stay persistent, if you don't give up, if you're unyielding and unhesitating in your values and your principles, you can win. . . . The lesson I took from all that is you can face the darkest of forces or face the most vicious of opposition," he says, "but if your cause is righteous, and if you try to stay worthy of that cause-which is a daily struggle-you can be victorious, you can accomplish your hopes and dreams."

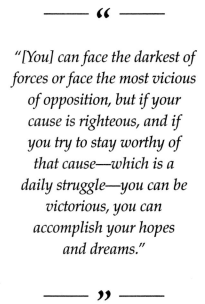

"[You] can face the darkest of forces or face the most vicious of opposition, but if your cause is righteous, and if you try to stay worthy of that cause—which is a daily struggle—you can be victorious, you can accomplish your hopes and dreams."

HOME AND FAMILY

Booker is single, and he continues to live in the Brick Towers housing project that he moved into in the 1990s. He remains close with his parents, who assisted in his mayoral campaigns, and with his brother, Cary, who is a professor at Rutgers University.

HOBBIES AND OTHER INTERESTS

Booker is a big fan of science fiction movies and television programs and is especially fond of "Star Trek." He gave up watching television, however, after becoming mayor because he felt it took up too much of his time. A vegetarian, he exercises regularly and is known for going on early-morning runs through the city streets.

FURTHER READING

Periodicals

City Journal, Spring 2007
Current Biography, Feb. 2007

New York Times, Apr. 24, 2002, p.A1; Sep. 26, 2004, Section 14NJ, p.1; Oct. 19, 2006, p.A1; July 3, 2007, p.B1

Newark (NJ) Star Ledger, Apr. 28, 2002, New Jersey section, p.19; July 1, 2007, New Jersey section, p.17; Aug. 28, 2007, p.1

U.S. News & World Report, Apr. 24, 2006, p.35

Washington Post, July 3, 2006, p.C1

Online Articles

http://abcnews.go.com/US/wireStory?id=3496596
(ABC News/Associated Press, "Shootings Renew Mayor's Sense of Purpose," Aug. 18, 2007)

http://www.city-journal.org/html/17_2_cory_booker.html
(City Journal, "Cory Booker's Battle for Newark," Spring 2007)

http://www.marshallcurry.com
(Marshall Curry Productions, "Street Fight," undated

http://www.npr.org/templates/story/story.php?storyId=5625405
(National Public Radio Morning Edition, "New Black Leaders Must Innovate," Aug. 8, 2006)

http://www.npr.org/templates/story/story.php?storyId=5446231
(National Public Radio News & Notes, "Cory Booker Wins Newark's 'Street Fight,'" June 2, 2006)

http://topics.nytimes.com/top/reference/timestopics/people/b/cory_booker /index.html
(New York Times, "Times Topics: Cory Booker," multiple articles)

ADDRESS

Cory Booker
Mayor's Office
200 City Hall
920 Broad Street
Newark, NJ 07102

WORLD WIDE WEB SITES

http://www.corybooker.com
http://www.ci.newark.nj.us/City_Government/mayor-cory-booker.aspx

Vanessa Hudgens 1988-
American Actress and Singer
Star of Disney's *High School Musical*

BIRTH

Vanessa Anne Hudgens was born on December 14, 1988, in
Salinas, California. She was the first child of Greg Hudgens and
Gina Guangco, who manage her career. Her sister, Stella, is six
years younger and is also pursuing acting. Her family background helped set Hudgens up for stardom: her grandparents
were big band musicians, so she became interested in singing at
a young age. Her striking good looks come from her parents'
multiethnic background—her mother is Filipino, Chinese, and
Hispanic, while her father is Irish and Native American.

YOUTH

Hudgens spent her early childhood in a small town in Oregon. Because she demonstrated a talent for performing, her family moved to San Diego, California, so the eight-year-old Vanessa could take lessons in singing, dancing, acting, and piano. She earned several roles in local community theater productions, including performances of *Cinderella, The King and I, The Music Man,* and *The Wizard of Oz.* The experience convinced her she wanted to become an entertainer. "It wasn't that my parents were pushy or anything," Hudgens recalled. "They were actually the ones going, 'Are you sure you want to do this?' because they knew this was a tough business, and they were afraid I'd get hurt. So I was the one pushing them."

> "It wasn't that my parents were pushy or anything," Hudgens recalled. "They were actually the ones going, 'Are you sure you want to do this?' because they knew this was a tough business, and they were afraid I'd get hurt. So I was the one pushing them."

A chance audition landed the aspiring actress her first television commercial; a good friend was too sick to attend, so Hudgens took her place. Afterwards, her parents moved the family to Los Angeles to bring them closer to more acting opportunities. By the time she entered her teens she was making guest appearances on popular television series; at 14 she appeared in her first film. This led to her first leading role, in Disney's *High School Musical,* which established her as a young star to watch.

EDUCATION

As a working child actor, Hudgens stopped attending school after seventh grade so that she would have the flexibility to pursue acting jobs. Instead, she was home-schooled by her mother, who also teaches her younger sister. Hudgens earned her high school equivalency in 2007, shortly after turning 18. She has stated that some day she would like to go to college, but she hasn't yet chosen a college or a date to begin her studies.

CAREER HIGHLIGHTS

Starting Out in Supporting Roles

In 2002 Hudgens earned a couple of one-episode guest appearances on the CBS shows "Still Standing" and "Robbery Homicide Division." The following year she won her first film role, playing a small supporting part in *Thirteen*. This hard-hitting drama focused on 13-year-old Tracy, played by Evan Rachel Wood, who falls into shoplifting and other risky behaviors. It also featured an Oscar-nominated performance by Holly Hunter. Hudgens played Noel, the wholesome friend whom Tracy shuns after getting in with the "cool" crowd. While the film didn't perform well at the box office, it did earn awards at several film festivals and gave Hudgens her first experience with film.

In 2004, Hudgens earned a larger role in *Thunderbirds*, a kids' action movie based on the classic British television show. Alan Tracy is the youngest member of a wealthy family that uses their spectacular vehicles, the Thunderbirds, to respond to disasters all over the world. Alan wants to be part of the International Rescue team, but his father thinks he is too young. When a villain traps the older Tracys on their space station, it's up to Alan and his two friends, Fermat and Tintin (played by Hudgens) to thwart his plans. A *Hollywood Reporter* critic called the three young actors "all appealing," and found the film "a piece of whiz-bang children's entertainment that could appeal to the family market far and wide."

> *While filming* **High School Musical,** *the cast spent months practicing their dance steps and recording vocals.* "We all lived in each other's pockets for the whole year," Hudgens recalled, "and we became a sort of family."

Hudgens continued finding steady work with guest appearances on television. In 2005 she appeared on the Fox sitcom "Quintuplets," while in 2006 she appeared in an episode of Nickelodeon's "Drake and Josh." She also found work on the Disney Channel, with a recurring guest role on "The Suite Life of Zack and Cody." In this comedy about twin brothers living in a luxury hotel, Hudgens appeared as part of their circle of friends.

During this time, Hudgens got the opportunity to audition for an upcoming Disney Channel movie that would revive the classic musical genre. When she read the script, the actress recalled, she got "crazy excited because it was everything I loved in one movie." After gaining the role, she and her co-stars spent months practicing their dance steps and recording vocals. "We all lived in each other's pockets for the whole year, and we became a sort of family." Their hard work and closeness paid off when the film, *High School Musical,* debuted in January 2006.

The *High School Musical* Phenomenon

High School Musical begins as two teens on vacation are forced to sing karaoke together at a New Year's Eve party. Bookish Gabriella Montez (played by Hudgens) and athletic Troy Bolton (played by Zac Efron) enjoy their duet, although neither has done much singing before. When Gabriella transfers to Troy's high school, the two of them think about trying out for the school musical, although this goes against their friends' expectations. When their musical rivals, twins Sharpay and Ryan, scheme to get Troy's big basketball game and Gabriella's scholastic decathlon scheduled for the same time as the musical callbacks, their friends come together to get them to the theater on time.

———— **"** ————

"I think young people are deprived of musicals they can relate to," Hudgens said to explain the popularity of High School Musical. *"When I was growing up I'd watch them all the time, but now there are very few out there for kids, and I'm just glad we brought the genre back in the way that we did."*

———— **"** ————

The premiere of *High School Musical* in January 2006 was an instant success; it brought a then-record 7.7 million viewers for a Disney Channel movie and was the highest non-sports cable broadcast of the month. Later airings brought in nearly 20 million more viewers in the U.S. alone. Worldwide it has been shown in over 100 countries, drawing over 170 million fans. In addition, the DVD of the film sold nearly eight million copies.

High School Musical also found unprecedented success on the music charts. The soundtrack hit No. 1, with over four million copies sold in the U.S., and was the top-selling CD in 2006. The soundtrack spawned several hit singles; the best-performing was a duet between Hudgens and Efron, "Breaking Free," which hit No. 4 on the Billboard Hot 100 and was the fastest moving single on the chart in 48 years. Another duet, "Start of Something New," hit No. 28, while her solo, "When There Was Me and You," charted at No. 71.

The show won several awards, including an Emmy for Outstanding Children's Program and a Teen Choice Award for Choice Comedy/Musical

High School Musical *was a huge hit on DVD.*

Program. Hudgens's turn as Gabriella Montez brought her recognition as well. She was nominated for a Teen Choice Award for TV Breakout Star, but lost to costar Efron; the two of them earned the Teen Choice Award for TV Chemistry. She was also nominated for best television actress by the Imagen Awards, which celebrate positive portrayals of Latinos.

> ———— " ————
>
> *"Just being on the tour bus is like a school field trip—when you're on the school bus and you're heading there and everybody is just having a blast, singing songs and everything."*
>
> ———— " ————

Hudgens was amazed by the runaway success of *High School Musical.* "I had no idea that [it] was going to be so huge," she said. When asked to explain it, she remarked, "I think young people are deprived of musicals they can relate to. When I was growing up I'd watch them all the time, but now there are very few out there for kids, and I'm just glad we brought the genre back in the way that we did." She and her co-stars also brought the musical to their fans in person. They sold out a concert tour of over 40 North American cities, with over 620,000 tickets sold. A DVD of the Houston show also became a hot seller. Hudgens not only got to re-create her numbers from *High School Musical,* she got a chance to showcase herself as a solo artist. "Her powerful vocals and magnetic smile set the crowd screaming," observed a reporter from the *San Jose Mercury News.*

Launching a Solo Album

Hudgens also used her popularity from *High School Musical* to begin building a recording career. She had offers from several companies, but chose to sign with Hollywood Records, a division of the Disney Company. It took her less than two months to record her first solo album, *V.* "The songs were already there, so I just went with the flow," she explained. *V*—the title refers to both "Vanessa" and "variety"—debuted in September 2006 and contained a mix of pop, rock, dance, and R&B songs. She sold 34,000 copies the first week, earning a respectable debut at No. 24 on the Billboard 200 album chart. Her first single, "Come Back to Me," debuted on MTV's "TRL" program and hit No. 18 on Billboard's Top 40 Mainstream chart. A second single, "Say OK," hit No. 47 on the Pop 100 chart. The album's combination of strong beats and teen-appropriate lyrics led some critics to call Hudgens a "baby J.Lo." By July 2007, *V* had been certified gold, with over 500,000 albums sold. The

Vanessa HUDGENS

Hudgens's first solo CD.

album also earned her a 2007 Teen Choice Award for Choice Music Breakout Artist: Female.

That fall and winter Hudgens went on tour in support of her album, performing concerts with the Cheetah Girls, a singing group with their own Disney Channel movies. Although traveling around the country and performing in a different place every night can be exhausting, she enjoyed the camaraderie with her fellow performers. "Just being on the tour bus is like a school field trip—when you're on the school bus and you're heading there and everybody is just having a blast, singing songs and everything."

High School Musical 2

After she finished touring, Hudgens rejoined the cast of *High School Musical* to film the sequel, *High School Musical 2*. With a bigger budget, the director and cast wanted to feature even more elaborate musical numbers. Luckily, the actress enjoys the dance numbers, although she admits dancing in heels can leave her feet aching. The set of *High School Musical 2* "was so crazy," Hudgens recalled. "Everything was way more chaotic because we really stepped it up."

In this sequel, school has let out for summer vacation, leading up to senior year. Troy and Gabriella get summer jobs working at the country club controlled by Sharpay's wealthy family. But things become tense as Sharpay schemes to break up Gabriella and Troy. Troy must decide whether to pursue the advantages that are available from Sharpay's wealthy family—even if it means neglecting Gabriella and his friends. It's a difficult summer, especially for Gabriella, but all is resolved as the group participates in the country club's annual talent show. The club's talent show provides a crucial decision for Troy—as well as the opportunity for more great song-and-dance numbers from the cast.

When the sequel aired in August 2007, its success showed the *High School Musical* phenomenon was still going strong. The first airing set a record as the most-watched basic cable telecast of all time, with over 17 million viewers. (Since many families held viewing parties, the actual number of viewers was most likely even higher.) It had more viewers than any broadcast program that week—in fact, it was the most-watched program on cable or broadcast television during the summer season.

The soundtrack *High School Musical 2* also fared well on the music charts. The soundtrack debuted at No. 1 on Billboard's Album chart, with 625,000 copies sold the first week alone. Its first single, the group number "What Time Is It," hit No. 6 on the Billboard Hot 100 chart. Three duets between Hudgens and Zac Efron also had strong single debuts: "You Are the Music in Me" was No. 9 on "Hot Digital Tracks" and debuted at No. 29 on the Pop 100; "Gotta Go My Own Way" placed on those same charts at No. 19 and No. 44; and "Everyday" reached No. 30 and No. 55.

Disney is already preparing for another sequel, this time as a motion picture, with plans to present *High School Musical 3* in theaters in 2008. Although as of fall 2007 Hudgens had yet to sign on to reprise her role as Gabriella, she has nothing but good words for her most famous role: "Gabriella is such a good role model that I'm not going to put her down in any way," the actress said. "[She is] a smart girl and she's into her studies, and yet she still gets the guy." It has also enabled Hudgens to reach a level of success that led *Forbes* magazine to place her in their Top 10 list of "Young Hollywood's Top-Earning Stars," with an estimated $2 million in earnings for 2006 alone.

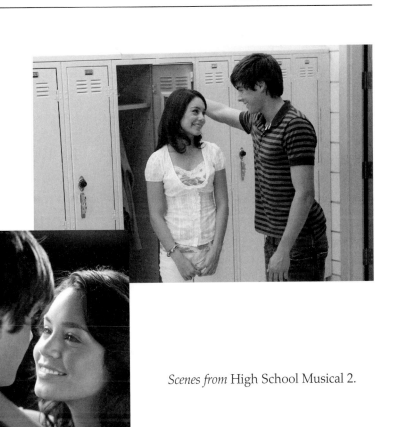

Scenes from High School Musical 2.

Even if Hudgens decided not to continue with the *High School Musical* franchise, she has plenty to keep her occupied. She's already planning to record her second solo album and perhaps write some songs for it. "I figured my first album I'll leave to the professionals," she said. "Once I know the process, I'll get my creative juices flowing." She also wouldn't mind taking on a more adult acting role, she says, "something more edgy that would be fulfilling as an actor." Her dream role would be to play and sing the part of Maria in the classic musical *West Side Story,* just as her idol, the late actress Natalie Wood, did in 1961.

—————— **"** ——————

"At times I wish I was a normal teenager. I never went to a real high school, to prom, or a high school football game," Hudgens said. But she also felt that the hard work and sacrifice has been worth it. "I gave it all up for my career, and it's going better than I could have wished. I made the right decision."

—————— **"** ——————

Hudgens is conscious that she has many young fans watching her future career. "Kids look up to the wrong people these days, not knowing right from wrong," she said. "I am honored to know kids are looking up to me." To those interested in following her into the entertainment business, she recommended, "Do all the school plays that you can, like theater and musicals. . . . . It's good experience!" Entertainment is "a hard business and there is a lot of rejection involved. But if you really want to do it, I'd say don't let anyone stop you!" Nevertheless, the actress admitted, "at times I wish I was a normal teenager. I never went to a real high school, to prom, or a high school football game." In the end, the hard work and sacrifice has been worth it, she said. "I gave it all up for my career, and it's going better than I could have wished. I made the right decision."

HOME AND FAMILY

Hudgens lives in Los Angeles with her family, which includes a toy poodle and other pets. She has been seen dating Zac Efron, her *High School Musical* co-star.

HOBBIES AND OTHER INTERESTS

Like any other teenager, Hudgens enjoys spending time with friends talking, shopping, or going to amusement parks. She also likes outdoor activities, such as hiking and camping. "I'm totally fine with not doing my hair or makeup, not taking a shower, and just hiking," she noted. Nevertheless, Hudgens knows how to take care of her appearance, and in 2007 she earned a contract as a celebrity spokesmodel for Neutrogena skin care products.

CREDITS

Film and Television

Thirteen, 2003
Thunderbirds, 2004
High School Musical, 2006 (TV movie)
High School Musical 2, 2007 (TV movie)

Recordings

High School Musical Soundtrack, 2006
V, 2006
High School Musical 2 Soundtrack, 2007

HONORS AND AWARDS

Teen Choice Awards: 2006, for TV Choice Chemistry for *High School Musical* (with Zac Efron); 2007, for Choice Music Breakout Artist-Female

FURTHER READING

Periodicals

Mail on Sunday (London), Dec. 3, 2006, p.46
Minneapolis Star-Tribune, Nov, 10, 2006, p.F1
New York Times, Mar. 11, 2007, sec.2, p.1
People, Summer 2007 (HSM2 Special), p.24; July 27, 2007, p. 8
San Jose Mercury News, Dec. 2. 2006
USA Today, Feb. 28, 2006, p.D4
Washington Post, Aug. 20, 2007, p.C1

Online Articles

http://www.hollywoodreporter.com
(Hollywood Reporter, review of *Thunderbirds,* July 20, 2004; "'High School Musical 2' Upstages TV Records," Aug. 19, 2007)
http://www.timeforkids.com
(Time for Kids, "Vanessa Hudgens Goes Solo," Nov. 7, 2006)

Online Databases

Biography Resource Center Online, 2007

ADDRESS

Vanessa Hudgens
Hollywood Records
500 South Buena Vista Street
Burbank, CA 91521

WORLD WIDE WEB SITES

http://hollywoodrecords.go.com/vanessahudgens
http://www.disney.go.com/disneychannel
http://www.myspace.com/vanessahudgens

Jennifer Hudson 1981-

American Singer and Actress
Winner of the 2007 Best Supporting Actress
Academy Award for *Dreamgirls*

BIRTH

Jennifer Kate Hudson was born on September 12, 1981, in Chicago, Illinois. Her mother, Darnell Hudson, is a secretary. The name of Hudson's father, who worked as a bus driver, is unclear; various sources have listed him as Samuel Simpson and Samuel Samson. The youngest of three children, Hudson has a brother, Jason, and a sister, Julia.

YOUTH

Hudson grew up in Englewood, on the southwest side of Chicago. "We were poor, but we weren't that poor—the house I grew up in had nine bedrooms," she said. In fact, she added, "we thought we were rich because we had everything we needed. My mother made sure we all did extracurricular activities to keep us busy. My brother James took piano lessons and I did ballet and modeled for the Sears catalogue when I was five."

An important part of their family life was worship at Pleasant Gift Missionary Baptist Church in Chicago, where Hudson developed her love of music. "I've known I wanted to sing since I was seven," she said. That was the age when she joined the church choir, singing alongside her sister Julia. "She liked it, I didn't," Julia Hudson recalled in an interview with *Vogue.* "When we were little girls, I was the tomboy, but she wanted style. When we could afford it, our mother took us to buy clothes and let us pick. I wanted pants. Jennifer always wanted the frilly skirt."

> "I'd ask for solos in church and they'd give me the runaround," she said. "I remember sitting in the bathroom of my house at seven years old crying and saying, 'Nobody will listen to me, so I'll listen to myself sing.'"

Not only did Hudson love to sing, she also craved an audience. "I'd ask for solos in church and they'd give me the runaround," she said. "I remember sitting in the bathroom of my house at seven years old crying and saying, 'Nobody will listen to me, so I'll listen to myself sing.'" But eventually, people did listen. One of the first people to notice and nurture her vocal talent was her maternal grandmother, Julia Kate Hudson, who was a prominent and inspirational singer at the Pleasant Gift Church. "They say I got my voice from my grandmother," Hudson recalled. "She just wanted to sing for the Lord in church. That's part of where I got my emotion from. I would hear her voice singing, 'How Great Thou Art.'"

It wasn't long before Hudson did get solos in church, giving rousing renditions that often brought the worshipers to tears. While still in elementary school, she was often asked to sing at family and friends' weddings and baptisms. She also performed in school musicals and talent shows, where audiences were astounded by her vocal range of six octaves.

Hudson attended Paul Laurence Dunbar Vocational Career Academy, a public high school in Chicago that offers students specialized career training in 22 vocations, including music. She was active in the school's chorus, which was directed by Richard Nunley. "[Hudson is] also a great classical singer and a lot of people don't know that," Nunley told the *Chicago Sun-Times.* "I wanted her to learn classical technique and develop a good instrument so she could be prepared to sing whatever music she wanted. She was crazy about Whitney Houston, Gladys Knight, Aretha Franklin-old school. She'd always say, 'Mr. Nunley, I'm going to make you proud of me. I'm going to be a famous singer.'" In city and state school singing competitions, Hudson always earned "superior" ratings.

At age 16, Hudson got a job at a local Burger King. She didn't stay there very long, as she preferred standing in the drive-thru practicing her singing rather than working on orders. Her last two years in high school were emotionally difficult, as she mourned the loss of her grandmother, Julia Kate Hudson, in 1998, and her father the following year.

Hudson graduated in 1999 from Paul Laurence Dunbar Vocational Career Academy, where she was voted "most talented" by the senior class. She enrolled in Langston University, in Langston, Oklahoma. But she left after a single semester, unhappy with the weather and homesick for Chicago. She then signed up for classes at Kennedy-King College, a community college in Chicago, and resumed singing with the Pleasant Gift choir.

After Hudson's daily performance on stage in **Big River**, *"there wouldn't be a dry eye in the house," said fellow performer Norissa Pearson. "Every night people cried, including the other actors."*

EARLY CAREER

Hudson's professional career began in 2001 with the help of her music teacher at Kennedy-King, who arranged an audition for her at a local production of *Big River,* a musical based on *The Adventures of Huckleberry Finn* by Mark Twain. Hudson's vocal skills at the audition were so impressive that she was hired on the spot. She didn't receive a speaking part, but she did get to showcase her talent by singing a solo, "How Blest We Are." After Hudson's daily performance on stage, "there wouldn't be a dry eye in the house," fellow performer Norissa Pearson told *Jet.* "Every night people cried, including the other actors."

Hudson's next job was on a Disney cruise ship, the *Disney Wonder.* She was the singing narrator of the musical *Hercules,* the story of the strong-man hero of Greek mythology. The production ran five or six days a week from February through August 2003. A self-described homebody, Hudson considered it a huge milestone in her life that she lived on a ship away from her family for almost seven months. "To be able to sing for 8,000 people a week is amazing," she said. "It's like, are you serious? You're paying me to do this? It was very exciting."

CAREER HIGHLIGHTS

"American Idol"

While Hudson was working on the cruise ship, her mother saw an advertisement that auditions were being held for the Fox network TV reality series "American Idol: Season 3." Darnell Hudson knew that her daughter dreamed about auditioning for the show, which gives aspiring singers a chance to sing on national television and jumpstart a singing career. At that point, in the summer of 2003, Hudson had a big decision to make: should she renew her contract with Disney Cruise Ships or should she leave and audition for "American Idol"? She decided on "Idol."

Hudson flew to Atlanta, Georgia, one of six cities in the U.S. where auditions were being held. After hours of waiting in line, it was finally her turn. She sang the Aretha Franklin hit "Share Your Love with Me," which was later shown on "Idol" in February 2004. The television judges—Paula Abdul, Simon Cowell, and Randy Jackson—all praised her voice. Jackson was the most enthusiastic, calling Hudson's rendition of the song "absolutely brilliant."

Once picked for the first round of semi-finals, Hudson flew to Hollywood, California, to continue in the competition. She sang "Imagine," by John Lennon, which the judges seemed to like, although they clearly weren't as bowled over as they were by her initial appearance. On the next night's results show, Hudson was not selected for the next round.

A Second Chance on "American Idol"

Hudson's stint on "Idol" would have been brief and forgotten by many if not for the Wild Card Round. For this part of "Idol," the judges Abdul,

Cowell, and Jackson each select a rejected contestant to bring back for another chance, with a fourth singer selected by popular vote. Hudson was Randy Jackson's Wild Card choice. Thrilled to be back on the show weeks after she was initially booted off, Hudson sang the Whitney Houston hit, "I Believe in You and Me." While Hudson had to endure some biting criticism from the notoriously tough judge Cowell about her choice of clothing, all the judges liked her vocal performance and she made it to the next round.

Over the next several weeks, the "American Idol" contestants prepared a different song from a specific musical genre for each week's

Hudson competing during "American Idol."

show. Hudson continued to impress just about everyone but Cowell. After her rendition of "Baby I Love You" by Aretha Franklin for Soul Week, Cowell told Hudson he thought that the song was a bad choice and criticized her for "oversinging" it. Abdul and Jackson disagreed, and both warmly praised Hudson's performance. For Country Week, Hudson chose "No One Else on Earth" by Wynonna Judd, and Cowell's criticism was even more caustic: "Let me sum this up for you. I think you are out of your depth in this competition." The studio audience booed Cowell's remarks, and Abdul and Jackson came to Hudson's defense yet again, praising her ability to belt out a song.

Despite Cowell's lack of enthusiasm, Hudson stayed in the competition with her performances of "No One Else on Earth" by Wynonna Judd for Country Week, and "(Love Is Like a) Heat Wave," made famous by Martha and the Vandellas, for Motown Week. One of Hudson's most memorable performances was her version of "Circle of Life," by Elton John. "Jennifer Hudson blew me away," said John, a guest judge that evening, after listening to all the contestants sing his compositions. "She sent chills up my spine. It was my favorite performance of the whole lot. . . . That voice is astonishing."

Hudson's rendition of the Whitney Houston hit "I Have Nothing" from the movie *The Bodyguard* for Movie Theme Week impressed the guest judge, the director Quentin Tarantino. "Hudson takes on Houston and wins!" Tarantino declared. By that point in the competition, even Cowell was coming around, telling Hudson, "You could be a front-runner."

On the episode aired on April 20, 2004, Hudson was won of seven singers left in the competition. She sang "Weekend in New England" by Barry Manilow. A guest judge on the show, Manilow told Hudson, "You took it all the way, sweetie. I loved it." Abdul, Cowell, and Jackson all agreed that she was becoming more confident with each song. Thrilled by her success, Hudson told Cowell, "I feel like I'm getting to be me now. This is Jenny's world."

> *One of Hudson's most memorable performances was her version of "Circle of Life," by Elton John. "Jennifer Hudson blew me away," said John, a guest judge that evening, after listening to all the contestants. "She sent chills up my spine. It was my favorite performance of the whole lot. . . . That voice is astonishing."*

Voted off "American Idol"

But the next night, the three singers with the least votes from television viewers were Hudson, Fantasia Barrino, and La Toya London. Many people were surprised and angry by this result, since these three women were widely considered to be the most talented contestants. The fact that all three are African American spurred some people, including an outraged Elton John, to dub the vote "incredibly racist." In the end, it was Hudson who was voted off the show.

A possible factor in Hudson's ouster was a Midwest storm that knocked out power to 15,000 homes in the Chicago area the night she was voted off "American Idol." Hudson was a favorite in her hometown, and many of her fans didn't see the show because of the outage. Ryan Seacrest, the show's host, had another theory—most people thought Hudson was such a shoo-in that they didn't bother to vote. After the final tally was announced, Seacrest reminded television viewers that they had to vote for their favorites every week. "You cannot let talent like this slip through the cracks," he said. A short time later, Fantasia Barrino ultimately won the competition.

Hudson has been asked many times how she felt about her loss on "American Idol." "I never felt it had anything to do with racism because I

Contestents performing on the "American Idol" grand finale (from left): Hudson, Fantasia Barrino, La Toya London, and Diana DeGarmo.

don't feel like I have a color," she reflected in an interview two years later. "Of course I was hurt. Oh, I cried. But clearly God had a greater plan for me."

As for Cowell, Hudson professed no hard feelings about his comments. Several years later, after she was nominated for an Academy Award for *Dreamgirls,* she had this to say. "I like Simon, he was always my favorite judge," she said. "He never criticized my weight, just my wardrobe. And looking back, I'm glad I was eliminated, because I don't think I'd be here if I had been the 'American Idol.' But I did tell Simon then that it wasn't over and I'd be back, so maybe now I could say, 'I told you so.'"

Dreamgirls

After the finale of "American Idol: Season 3," the 10 finalists, including Hudson, went on a 48-city tour. She was a guest star on the TV show "On Air with Ryan Seacrest," singing a duet with Barry Manilow, and she performed at several benefit concerts. Then, in May 2005, Hudson got a call at her Chicago home asking her to audition for the role of Effie in the movie version of the Broadway musical *Dreamgirls*.

Dreamgirls is the story of a singing group formed in the 1960s by Effie White, the lead singer, and her best friends Deena Jones and Lorrell Robinson. They meet Curtis Taylor Jr. at a local talent show. He becomes their manager and arranges for them to be a backup act for James "Thunder" Early, a rhythm and blues star. Eventually, Taylor turns the Dreamettes into the Dreams, a pop music act, with Deena as the lead singer. Deena, who is slender, also replaces Effie, who is heavier, as Taylor's love interest. Effie quits the group and ends up as a single mother trying to survive on her own. She tries to make a comeback years later, recording a song written by her brother. But Taylor attempts to stymie her success by arranging for Deena to record the same song. In the end, Deena sees through Taylor's manipulations, and she and Effie are finally reconciled.

> — **"** —
>
> *"I like Simon, he was always my favorite judge," she said. "He never criticized my weight, just my wardrobe. And looking back, I'm glad I was eliminated, because I don't think I'd be here if I had been the 'American Idol.' But I did tell Simon then that it wasn't over and I'd be back, so maybe now I could say, 'I told you so.'"*
>
> — **"** —

Dreamgirls opened on Broadway in 1981 and was a smash hit. The show won six Tony Awards, including Best Actress in a Musical for Jennifer Holliday, whose portrayal of Effie was widely acclaimed. Many people who saw the show thought the role of Effie was based on the singer Florence Ballard, who started the real-life 1960s trio called the Supremes. Ballard was eventually fired from the group and replaced as lead singer by Diana Ross. Ross went on to have a successful career as a solo singer and actress, while Ballard became impoverished and died of a heart attack at age 32. The creators of *Dreamgirls* have said that the story is fictional, and Ross has angrily denied in interviews she was in any way like the character of Deena.

For the new movie version of *Dreamgirls*, almost 800 young women tried out for the role of Effie, including Fantasia Barrino, winner of "American Idol: Season 3." "The casting of Effie was crucial," said Bill Condon, the director and screenwriter of *Dreamgirls*. "If we had made a mistake, it would have been impossible to overcome." Hudson actually had three auditions

Hudson in scenes from Dreamgirls: *with Jamie Foxx (top); with Beyoncé Knowles (center); and with Eddie Murphy, Beyoncé Knowles, and Anika Noni Rose (bottom).*

for the role over a six-month period. Condon and the movie's producers were concerned about her lack of acting experience. Her final on-camera screen test, however, proved to be convincing. Condon called her to say, "Congratulations, you're our Effie White." Recalling that moment, Hudson said, "I shouted, I hit the floor, I thanked Jesus. I celebrated for ten minutes, then I said, 'I got to focus.'"

The other lead roles in *Dreamgirls* were played by Jamie Foxx as Curtis Taylor, Beyoncé Knowles as Deena, Eddie Murphy as James "Thunder" Early, and Danny Glover as Marty Madison—all established movie stars and seasoned performers. Meeting them for the first time, at a read-through of the script, made Hudson feel nervous. "I was afraid they were all thinking, 'How is this little girl gonna play this role? She's not experienced like we are,'" Hudson recalled. "But it wasn't like that at all. They were very supportive and patient and helpful."

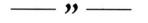

> "The casting of Effie was crucial," said Bill Condon, the director and screenwriter of **Dreamgirls**. "If we had made a mistake, it would have been impossible to overcome."

Becoming Effie

Hudson was instructed to pack on extra weight to play Effie, which she did by eating cookies, cakes, and pies. She went from a size 12 to a size 16. Gaining 25 pounds wasn't nearly as hard for Hudson as Condon's requirement that she become temperamental and isolate herself from the other actors in order to better portray Effie's tough nature. Condon's "Diva 101 course," as Hudson put it, "took some getting adjusted to, but it was part of Effie that was needed, that he felt I didn't have and that I needed to tap into."

Another hurdle for Hudson was preparing herself for her love scenes with Jamie Foxx, not all of which were included in the final cut of the movie. Playing Curtis Taylor, Foxx tried his best to make her feel comfortable, and Hudson got over her jitters by letting the action in the movie take over. "After a while it became Effie and Curtis, not Jennifer and Jamie," she said. As the story of *Dreamgirls* progresses, Effie faces the rejection of Curtis as well as her singing group. That's when Effie belts out "And I Am Telling You I'm Not Going," a highly emotional and defiant response to being cast aside. The song is the linchpin of the movie, and Hudson said she thought of Florence Ballard, the rejected, real-life Supreme, when she sang the song. "In reading [about Ballard] I got angry for Florence," Hudson said. "Like highly upset. Like, oooh, and I felt like her voice."

Hudson could identify with Effie because of her experience on "American Idol." "Effie was told that she was no good and couldn't make it either," she said. "She was cast aside. But in the end we both prevail. I like that."

Dreamgirls opened in December 2006 to mostly excellent reviews. Many of the critics singled out Hudson for praise. "The film is worth seeing simply for the on-screen splendor of Hudson, a losing contestant on TV's 'American Idol,'" Claudia Puig wrote in *USA Today.* "She's a natural—musically and theatrically—and delivers a tour-de-force performance." Another great review appeared in the *New York Times.* "The dramatic and musical peak of *Dreamgirls*—the showstopper, the main reason to see the movie—comes around midpoint, when Jennifer Hudson, playing Effie White, sings 'And I Am Telling You I'm Not Going,'" wrote reviewer A.O. Scott. "That song has been this musical's calling card since the first Broadway production 25 years ago, but to see Ms. Hudson tear into it on screen nonetheless brings the goose-bumped thrill of witnessing something new, even historic."

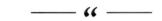

Hudson could identify with Effie because of her experience on "American Idol." "Effie was told that she was no good and couldn't make it either," she said. "She was cast aside. But in the end we both prevail. I like that."

Winning the Golden Globe and the Oscar

Not long after the film opened, the nominations for the 2007 Golden Globe awards were announced, and Hudson's name was on the list for the award for Best Supporting Actress. She won, and made a tearful acceptance speech in which she said, "I had always dreamed, but I never dreamed this big. This goes far beyond anything I could ever have imagined." But for Hudson, the dreams got even bigger. She was also nominated for an Academy Award (Oscar), and at the awards ceremony in February 2007 she heard her name called as the winner of the award for Best Supporting Actress. A visibly shaken Hudson asked the audience for a moment so she could compose herself. "I didn't think I was going to win but, wow, if my grandmother was here to see me now," she said. "She was my biggest inspiration for everything because she was a singer and she

Winning the Academy Award for
Best Supporting Actress was a wonderful shock for Hudson.

had the passion for it but she never had the chance. And that was the thing that pushed me forward to continue."

In October 2006, Hudson signed a record deal with the veteran musical producer Clive Davis. She spent six months recording songs for her debut album, which will appear on J Records, a division of Arista. Hudson has also pursued her acting career, working with fellow Oscar winner Forest Whitaker in the film *Winged Creatures*, due to be released in 2008. "I don't want to do just musicals," she remarked. "I want to experiment and do different things and exercise that acting muscle. I'm a firm believer in using what God gives you to make your living. Singing is Number 1, and now it's singing and acting."

HOME AND FAMILY

Hudson lives in a four-bedroom co-op in Hyde Park, a neighborhood of Chicago. "I've always wanted to live in Hyde Park, so that's where I'm going to be," she said. "Of course they're like, 'You should move to L.A., New York,' but I want my first place to be here at home in Chicago. There's no other place in the world like it. It's where my family is." Hudson met her boyfriend, James Payton, a maintenance engineer, in Chicago when she was 13, and they've been together ever since. "He was my brother's best friend," she said.

HOBBIES AND OTHER INTERESTS

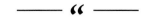

Hudson is proud of her body size. "Why should I feel like the minority when the majority of America is a size 12?" she remarked. "Plus a lot of singers don't sound the same when they lose weight. . . . Hey, somebody has to represent the big girls. Why not me?"

Hudson likes to draw in her spare time. She enjoys going to church, which is still her favorite place to sing. She is proud of her clean-cut image. "I don't smoke and I don't do drugs," she said. "I never have and I never plan on it." She is also proud of her body size. "Why should I feel like the minority when the majority of America is a size 12?" she remarked. "Plus a lot of singers don't sound the same when they lose weight. I have a little singer's pouch, and that's where my voice comes from, so you're all just going to have to get used to my jelly. Hey, somebody has to represent the big girls. Why not me?"

CREDITS

Dreamgirls, 2006 (movie)
Dreamgirls, 2006 (soundtrack)

HONORS AND AWARDS

National Board of Review Awards: 2006, Breakthrough Performance (Female), for *Dreamgirls*
New York Film Critics Circle Awards: 2006, Best Supporting Actress, for *Dreamgirls*
ShoWest Awards: 2006, Female Star of Tomorrow
Academy Awards: 2007, Best Supporting Actress, for *Dreamgirls*

British Academy of Film and Television Arts Awards (BAFTA): 2007, Best
 Actress in a Supporting Role, for *Dreamgirls*
BET Awards: 2007 (2 awards), Best New Artist and Best Actress, for
 Dreamgirls
Broadcast Film Critics Association Awards: 2007, Best Supporting Actress,
 for *Dreamgirls*
Golden Globe Awards: 2007, Best Supporting Actress, for *Dreamgirls*
Screen Actors Guild Awards: Outstanding Performance by a Female Actor
 in a Supporting Role, for *Dreamgirls:* 2007
Teen Choice Awards: 2007, Choice Movie Actress-Drama, for *Dreamgirls*

FURTHER READING

Books

West, Betsy. *Jennifer Hudson American Dream Girl: An Unauthorized
 Biography,* 2007

Periodicals

Chicago Sun Times, Dec. 17, 2006, p.D1
Chicago Tribune, Dec. 17, 2006, p.C1
Essence, Mar. 2007, p.129
Evening Standard (London), Jan. 25, 2007, p.32
Los Angeles Times, Dec. 4, 2006, p.E1
Minneapolis Star Tribune, Apr. 29, 2007, p.F1
New York Post, Feb. 25, 2007, p.38
New York Times, Dec. 15, 2006, p.E1
Newsweek, Dec. 11, 2006, p.96
San Francisco Chronicle, Dec. 10, 2006, Sunday Datebook, p.19
Toronto Star, Dec. 24, 2006, p.S10
USA Today, Dec. 15, 2006, p.D1
Vogue, Mar. 2007, p.542

ADDRESS

Jennifer Hudson
J Records
745 Fifth Avenue
New York, NY 10151

WORLD WIDE WEB SITES

http://www.myspace.com/jenniferhudson
http://www.hollywood.com/celebrity/Jennifer_Hudson/1745865
http://www.dreamgirlsmovie.com

BRIEF ENTRY
Zach Hunter 1991-
American Anti-Slavery Activist
Founder of Loose Change to Loosen Chains and
Author of *Be the Change*

EARLY YEARS

Zach Hunter was born in 1991 in Washington State. His parents are Gregg and Penny Hunter. His father is the vice president of public affairs for a non-profit organization. His mother is a marketing consultant. Zach has one sibling, Nate, who is seven years younger. Zach attended the Christian Fellowship

School in Ashburn, Virginia, but later transferred to the Providence Christian Academy in Lilburn, Georgia, located in suburban Atlanta. He lives in Suwanee, another suburb of Atlanta. In fall 2007, he entered the tenth grade. He has been a good student in school, getting mostly A's and B's. He enjoys playing tennis, listening to music, and reading.

MAJOR ACCOMPLISHMENTS

Twenty-First Century Slavery

Zach was 12 years old and in the seventh grade when he learned that even though slavery has long been outlawed, the modern world still supports the business of buying and selling human beings. He first became aware of this during Black History Month (February), when his school curriculum included information about the history of slavery. He learned about William Wilberforce, a member of the British Parliament during the 1800s who, although he had once been a slave trader, later fought long and hard to abolish slavery in England. He learned about Harriet Tubman, a former slave who led hundreds of people on a dangerous flight from slavery in the American South to freedom in the North and in Canada. He learned about Frederick Douglass, an African American who was born into slavery. Douglass later became one of the driving forces behind the American abolitionist movement of the 1800s, which sought to wipe out slavery and slave trade. One of Zach's favorite books is *The Diary of Frederick Douglass.*

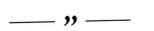

> *According to statistics from the United Nations, about 27 million people now live as slaves worldwide, with some 200,000 of them held captive in the United States. Roughly half of those counted as slaves are children.*

Zach was inspired by these heroes and felt that if he had been alive during the 1800s, he would certainly have joined them in their fight against slavery. Then he learned that slavery still exists and is even thriving in the modern world. The trans-Atlantic slave trade was abolished in 1807, and slavery was outlawed in the United States in 1865 and declared illegal worldwide by the United Nations in 1948. Yet, the proportion of the world's people who live as slaves today is actually higher than it was in the days of legal enslavement. According to statistics from the United Nations, about 27 million people now live as slaves worldwide, with some 200,000 of them held captive in the United States. Roughly half of those counted as slaves are children.

Although their bondage has no legal basis, these people are physically imprisoned or held by threats of violence against themselves or their family members. They are often tricked by false information about good jobs in faraway locations. Then when they travel long distances in search of these jobs, they are kidnapped or trapped. Their official identification papers may be taken from them, and they are then forced to work for the benefit of others, with no pay or other benefit to themselves. They may be told that they will be allowed to return home someday, but only after they have "earned" the freedom that was stolen from them. In some places, entire families are enslaved by unfair lending practices that force generations into unpaid work in order to pay off a debt. The jobs they must do are frequently dangerous, and they work long hours in conditions that are inhumane. Slaves are often imprisoned and used until they can no longer be productively exploited, then simply abandoned or are forced to work until they die.

"It's sickening that people are still owning other people and using them to do their work," he said. *"It made me feel bad. But I didn't think it was enough just to feel bad. If I just had those emotions and didn't do anything with them then they would pretty much be worthless."*

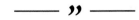

Zach was shocked to learn the truth about modern slavery. "It's sickening that people are still owning other people and using them to do their work," he said. "It made me feel bad. But I didn't think it was enough just to feel bad. If I just had those emotions and didn't do anything with them then they would pretty much be worthless."

Loose Change to Loosen Chains

Zach pondered what one teenager could do about the huge problem of global slavery. In a way the problem is harder to fight now than it was in the 1800s, because slavery is illegal and thus is more hidden from view. For help he turned to his mother, Penny Hunter, who then worked for the International Justice Mission (IJM), an organization that fights slavery as part of its overall mission to protect basic human rights around the world. Zach learned that in addition to the IJM, there are other modern organizations like Free the Slaves, Rugmark, and others that work to expose and smash

Students working to raise money for Loose Change to Loosen Chains.
(Photo Credit: Ted Haddock/International Justice Mission®)

slavery rings. He wanted to do whatever he could to support the work of these anti-slavery organizations, and most importantly, he wanted to alert other people to the reality that slavery does exist in the world today.

Zach hoped to accomplish both these goals with a program called Loose Change to Loosen Chains (LC2LC). According to *Real Simple* magazine, there may be as much as $10.5 billion lying around American homes in the form of loose change. Zach asked his classmates at the Christian Fellowship School in Ashburn, Virginia, to search their homes for loose change and bring it in to a fundraising drive at school. By doing so, they would raise money to donate to anti-slavery activist groups, and they would also raise awareness of this terrible problem. His initial drive was a success, bringing in more than $8,500 in just a little more than a month.

Zach wanted to do much more. He widened the scope of LC2LC by inviting other students around the world to set up similar drives in their schools, churches, and youth groups, using simple plastic cups to collect the change. He kept things simple and local. He provided those who wanted to help with the information they needed, entrusted them with the responsibility of handling the funds they collected, and let them decide which activist group would receive the cash they raised. Because of this approach, it is difficult to say how much LC2LC fundraising has now contributed toward the cause of abolishing slavery, but Zach has personally raised more than $20,000.

Talking about the success of LC2LC, Zach reflected, "I decided to take something as underestimated as loose change [and] as underestimated as the teenage years, [and] put them together. This is an important issue for my generation. Thanks to the media we have seen suffering up close and many of us feel compelled to do something about it. The main plan is to abolish slavery within my lifetime and I really believe that that can happen. This Loose Change to Loosen Chains campaign is really in my heart. It is something I am passionate about. People my age can really change things. It is sort of my dream for my generation."

Becoming a Public Speaker

Zach's commitment to fighting slavery didn't end with his creation of LC2LC. At about the same time as Zach was starting his abolitionist efforts, the life story of the British abolitionist William Wilberforce was released as the film *Amazing Grace*. The film led to several anti-slavery actions, including The Amazing Change Campaign and The Better Hour—both movements designed to raise awareness about modern slavery and bring it to an end. Hunter became the youth spokesman for both and The Amazing Change Campaign and The Better Hour. With The Amazing Change Campaign, he became an energetic promoter of their anti-slavery petition and presented it at a White House Policy Roundtable on Human Trafficking. There were more than 100,000 signatures on the petition, mostly those of students like Zach.

———— **"** ————

"I decided to take something as underestimated as loose change [and] as underestimated as the teenage years, [and] put them together. This is an important issue for my generation. Thanks to the media we have seen suffering up close and many of us feel compelled to do something about it."

———— **"** ————

Just a few years before he founded LC2LC, Zach had been considered a shy child. "I was deathly afraid to get up in front of a class and do a book report," he recalled. He had even struggled with an anxiety disorder that sometimes left him feeling weak and nauseated. Taking his message about slavery to the world, Zach now speaks to groups ranging from school assemblies to huge crowds at music festivals and other events. He has even appeared on national television several times and has been honored as a modern day hero by CNN. A Christian, he gives God credit for

Hunter speaking to students at a music festival in Wisconsin.
(Photo Credit: Ted Haddock/International Justice Mission®)

his newfound self-confidence. He recalled one incident where he felt very afraid to get up before the crowd he was supposed to address, and his mother told him that it was okay to back out of the commitment. He considered doing so for a moment, then realized that if he gave in to his nervousness, the message that slavery needs to be fought would fail to reach the people in that large audience. Zach went on stage. Now, he said, "I don't usually get nervous speaking," and he has spoken to hundreds of thousands of people.

Graphic Stories about Slavery

When Zach gives a speech, he tries to reach the hearts of his listeners. He holds up a pair of small shackles designed to be locked around the ankles of a child who might be no more than five years old. These are not historical artifacts from a museum, but real tools used to enslave people today, he points out. "What if it were you, or your best friend, or your brother, or your mom?" he asked. "What if your feet were shackled together all day long as you sit on a dirt floor rolling cigarettes? What if you had to dive down to the bottom of the river to untangle your masters' fishing nets, after your best friend had just drowned the day before doing the same thing?"

Zach often tells the story of Rakesh, an Indian boy who was kept captive in a rug factory. Rakesh and other children were kept from school and forced to work on the looms, which have strings stretched so tight that the workers' fingers are frequently cut and bloody from working with them. Thanks to the efforts of modern abolitionists, Rakesh and his fellow child-slaves were freed. Zach tells of children enslaved because their parents were too poor to feed them or were in debt. He tells of entire families who work all day long crushing boulders into gravel or making bricks in red-hot kilns. He tells of the many children who are forced to work as servants, soldiers, and even prostitutes.

His busy public speaking schedule means that Zach sometimes has to miss school. While some of his teachers are supportive, it can still be very difficult to keep up, so his parents have tried to limit his travel to weekends and summers. He works hard to balance his priorities at school with his desire to change the world.

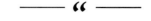

> *"What if it were you, or your best friend, or your brother, or your mom?" Hunter asked. "What if your feet were shackled together all day long as you sit on a dirt floor rolling cigarettes? What if you had to dive down to the bottom of the river to untangle your masters' fishing nets, after your best friend had just drowned the day before doing the same thing?"*

Zach's Book: *Be the Change*

Trying to extend the reach of his message even further, Zach published a book in 2007. *Be the Change: Your Guide to Freeing Slaves and Changing the World* is full of facts, short entries about inspirational people from the past and present, and large and small ideas for making positive changes in the world. Quotes from Wilberforce and other early abolitionists are side-by-side with narratives from people who have escaped modern-day slavery, and there is also material that is not specifically about slavery, but simply about using passion to do great things.

"It's about world-changers . . . people who have really made a difference," Zach said of his book. "It's to inspire kids to get involved. I have questions at the end and personal reflections about it. Each of the chapters has a theme like courage or influence or compassion. It's geared toward teens but I'd be glad to have anyone read it." Zach is also working on his second book, *Generation: Change,* which is scheduled to come out in 2008. In addition, he blogs for *Breakaway Magazine.*

Future Plans

In addition to carrying on with school, his public speaking, and his work with LC2LC, Zach hopes to travel to India or Africa soon and also to film a documentary. He passionately hopes that many people will get involved in spreading the message about modern slavery. "Just get educated," he urged. "Tell everyone you know about it. Information is one of the most powerful tools against slavery." Although the issue of slavery is the most important one to him, he knows that it is vital for people to work on other issues as well. "There are so many great things out there, but I usually encourage people to just get involved with one specific thing. It can be very overwhelming to take on a lot of causes at once. I encourage people to find one cause they are passionate about and dedicate their lives to that."

> *Hunter passionately hopes that many people will get involved in spreading the message about modern slavery. "Just get educated," he urged. "Tell everyone you know about it. Information is one of the most powerful tools against slavery."*

Zach has great faith in the ability of teenagers to get things done. "I believe that we can be written about in the history books as a generation that put ourselves behind and thought of other people instead of ourselves," he stated. Sometimes the special power of young people comes directly from their lack of experience, he explained: "As you get older, you become more familiar with reality, and it just doesn't seem realistic that you can abolish slavery." Creating LC2LC as a student-led movement was, in part, because "adults, as nice as they are, can sometimes be wet blankets. But since students are resource-poor and have passion, and adults are often passion-poor and have resources, together we can be a deadly combination."

WRITINGS

Be the Change: Your Guide to Freeing Slaves and Changing the World, 2007

THE AMAZING
CHANGE

A portion of the proceeds
will help end modern-day
slavery.

Be the Change

Your Guide to Freeing Slaves and
Changing the World

Zach Hunter

Includes a letter from Jon Foreman of **Switchfoot**

*Zach's book is a guide for others interested in
learning more about slavery and abolition.*

FURTHER READING

Books

Hunter, Zach. *Be the Change: Your Guide to Freeing Slaves and Changing the World,* 2007

Periodicals

Atlanta Journal-Constitution, Feb. 25, 2007
Christian Science Monitor, Feb. 21, 2007

Online Articles

http://www.abcnews.go.com
   (ABC News, transcript of interview with Zach Hunter from *Good Morning America,* Mar. 15, 2007)
http://www.christiantoday.com
   (Christian Today, "Meet Zach Hunter-The Teenage Abolitionist," Feb. 22, 2007)
http://www.cnn.com/SPECIALS/2007/cnn.heroes
   (CNN.com, "CNN Heroes Gallery: Young Wonder," no date)
http://www.publishersweekly.com
   (Publishers Weekly Online, "Abolitionist Teen Speaks out against Modern-Day Slavery," Feb. 21, 2007)

ADDRESS

Zach Hunter
Zondervan Publishing
5300 Patterson Avenue SE
Grand Rapids, MI 49530

WORLD WIDE WEB SITES

http://www.myspace.com/lc2lc
http://www.lc2lc.com

JONAS BROTHERS
Kevin Jonas 1987-
Joseph Jonas 1989-
Nick Jonas 1992-
American Rock Band

BIRTH

The Jonas Brothers band includes three members: Paul Kevin Jonas, known as Kevin, was born on November 5, 1987, in Teaneck, New Jersey; Joseph Adam Jonas was born on August 15, 1989, in Casa Grande, Arizona; and Nicholas Jerry Jonas, known as Nick, was born on September 16, 1992, in Dallas, Texas. They also have a younger brother, Frankie, whom they call "the bonus Jonas." Frankie is eight years younger than

Nick. Their father, Kevin Jonas, is an evangelical minister. He was the co-founder of Christ for the Nations Music and also served as a worship leader for that organization in Dallas. He was later pastor of an Assembly of God church in Wyckoff, New Jersey. Their mother, Denise Jonas, is a sign-language teacher.

YOUTH

The Jonas family lived in Wyckoff, New Jersey, for some years before the boys started their band. Wyckoff is close to New York City, where they spent a lot of time. Music has always been important in the Jonas family. Both parents sang church music, and the boys' father co-founded a Christian music ministry. Each of the brothers recalls feeling strongly drawn to performance at an early age. Kevin, the trio's lead guitarist, re-members being home sick from school, finding a guitar and a how-to-play book, and learning the basic chords after about three days of practicing. "The moment I picked up a guitar," he said, "that was the minute I knew I wanted to do this for the rest of my life." Nick says that from the time he was about two years old, he would wake up in the morning and start singing for the rest of the day. "I'd watch *Peter Pan,* the VHS of the Broadway version, and I'd have a temper tantrum if anybody turned it off," he said.

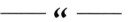

> *"The moment I picked up a guitar," Kevin said, "that was the minute I knew I wanted to do this for the rest of my life."*

EDUCATION

Before becoming a touring act, the Jonas Brothers attended the East Christian School in North Haledon, New Jersey. After they formed the band and became a touring act, they were homeschooled. Using curriculum from Accelerated Christian Education, they study with parents and tutors, juggling coursework with touring and rehearsing. Kevin, the eldest, has earned his diploma. Balancing the demand of performing with the demands of school is hard, said Nick, "but we find a way to get it done. You have to be really disciplined (about school work). We remember we have to get it done, but have a big opportunity, too, with music."

FIRST JOBS

Nick Jonas was at the barber for a haircut one day, and as usual, he was singing a song. Another customer at the shop heard him and was so impressed with his voice that she referred him to a talent manager. It wasn't long before Nick was landing roles in Broadway productions. Joseph Jonas, the middle brother, had aspired to be a member of a comedy troupe, but after seeing his younger brother in a Broadway musical, he decided to audition for stage roles, too. He soon won a part in Baz Luhrmann's Broadway production of the opera *La Boheme.* The Jonas brothers also worked together in television commercials, including advertisements for Burger King, Clorox bleach, LEGO toys, and Battle Bots.

Nick's strong vocal skills earned him roles in the casts of several Broadway shows, including *Annie Get Your Gun, Beauty and the Beast, A Christmas Carol,* and *Les Miserables.* It was his singing on a cast album of *Beauty and the Beast* that brought him to the attention of Johnny Wright, the man who had also created the pop bands Backstreet Boys and 'N Sync. Soon after that his solo demo CD landed on the desk of Steve Greenberg, the new president of Columbia Records.

Columbia signed Nick to a contract and began planning an album for this new talent. After hearing some songs Nick had written with Joseph and Kevin, record company representatives asked all three brothers to come

Balancing the demand of performing with the demands of school is hard, said Nick, "but we find a way to get it done. You have to be really disciplined (about school work). We remember we have to get it done, but have a big opportunity, too, with music."

for an audition. In the end, they signed a group contract. "I didn't like the record he'd made," Greenberg said about Nick's initial solo demo. "But his voice stuck out, so I met with him and found out he had two brothers." Greenberg had discovered Hanson, so he knew how to handle a family act. "I liked the idea of putting together this little garage-rock band and making a record that nodded to the Ramones and '70s punk. So Michael Mangini and I went into the studio with the Jonas Brothers and did it."

CAREER HIGHLIGHTS

In July 2005, the Jonas Brothers began performing as a band. Even though Nick and Joe had already faced major audiences on Broadway, performing in a rock band was a very different experience. They broke in their act with short sets at the Bloomfield Avenue Café in Montclair, New Jersey, and played their first full-length concert in Acton, Massachusetts. They also

Kevin, Nick, and Joe at the 2007 Teen Choice Awards.

toured and made appearances with other musical acts during the summer of 2005, including Jesse McCartney, Aly & AJ, the Veronicas, the Backstreet Boys, and the Click Five.

The boys' good looks undoubtedly won them some fans, but they also showed that they had legitimate musical talent from the start. They wrote their own songs, played their own instruments, and sang their own lyrics. The result was a high-energy sound that had a grunge/garage-band edge, with powerful guitar work from Kevin, catchy hooks, and strong harmonies. Lead vocals were shared by Nicholas and Joseph, while Kevin contributed backup.

The Jonas Brothers were very busy in 2006. In April, they released their first album, titled *It's About Time*. They also participated in the government campaign "What's Your Anti-Drug?" which took them to schools around the country. Late in the summer, they made an appearance at the Revelation Generation Christian Rock Festival in Frenchtown, New Jersey. In December, they went to Germany as part of a USO tour designed to reach children of military personnel, educating them about the music business and encouraging them to pursue their dreams. In addition, their music was featured in the made-for-TV Nickelodeon movie *Zoey 101: Spring Break-up*.

It's About Time

The Jonas Brothers' first CD, *It's About Time,* was released in 2006. They wrote about 60 songs before settling on the seven that, along with four tunes not written by them, made the final cut. Several of the songs had a time-related theme. For example, "7:05" is about the way the exact moment of meeting someone special might be etched in your mind. "Time for Me to Fly" celebrates reaching the moment when dreams come true. "Year 3000" is about meeting a time traveler, and "6 Minutes" reflects on the range of emotions that a person can go through in a very short time when attracted to somebody new. Other songs on the album included "Underdog," about an unpopular girl who will eventually go on to do great things in the world; "Dear God," a plea for guidance in life; and "Mandy," a tribute to a girl the boys knew in real life. Mandy had been Nick's best friend when they were younger and had dated Joe for a while. They made three different videos to support the hard-driving song, and the real Mandy even made an appearance.

Reviewing *It's About Time* for the *Virginian-Pilot,* Hilary Saunders called it "a surprisingly impressive debut" considering the young ages of the band members. Another reviewer, Angelique Moon, wrote in *Soundings:* "With its upbeat, catchy vibe, vocal harmonies, and mature, thought-provoking lyrics, it's a great choice to introduce listeners to this up-and-coming pop punk rock band. It'll be hard to not want to listen to the blend between Nick's strong powerhouse voice, Joseph's cooler, smooth rock pipes, and Kevin's killer guitar handlings."

As reviewer Angelique Moon wrote in **Soundings:** *"With its upbeat, catchy vibe, vocal harmonies, and mature, thought-provoking lyrics, it's a great choice to introduce listeners to this up-and-coming pop punk rock band. It'll be hard to not want to listen to the blend between Nick's strong powerhouse voice, Joseph's cooler, smooth rock pipes, and Kevin's killer guitar handlings."*

Despite the band's solid appeal and growing fan base, *It's About Time* didn't sell particularly well. Steve Greenberg, the executive at Columbia Records who had taken an interest in the band, had left the company. After that, there was little in the way of traditional promotion or radio airplay for the album. Only about 62,000 copies were sold, and *It's About Time* went out of print when the boys left Columbia to sign with Hollywood Records in 2007.

Disney Connection

Hollywood Records, the band's new home, is owned by Disney, a company that has proven its skill at promoting young stars. Raven-Symone, Miley Cyrus, and the Cheetah Girls are some of the company's success stories. The first project they worked on with Hollywood Records was "Kids of the Future," a remake of the song "Kids of America." It was to be used on the soundtrack for the Disney film *Meet the Robinsons.* According to Joe, making the video to go with that song "was cool because we shot the whole thing in front of a green-screen and they added the futuristic things behind us [later]."

Until then, the Jonas Brothers had received almost no airplay on traditional radio. Now, their music began to be heavily rotated on the satellite music channel, Radio Disney, and in videos featured on the Disney Channel. They also had a guest appearance on the popular Disney television program "Hannah Montana."

Jonas Brothers

In addition to being strongly promoted by Disney, the Jonas Brothers got even more publicity when it signed a multimillion-dollar deal to endorse

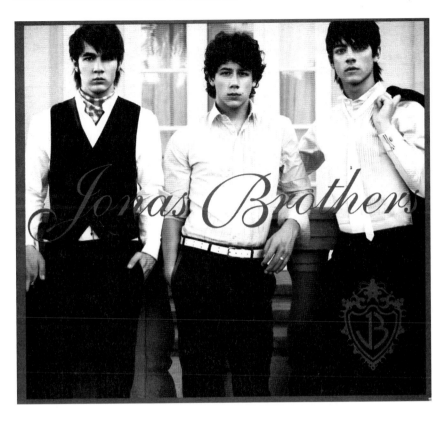

Their second CD, Jonas Brothers, *was a hit with fans and critics when released in 2007.*

the popular candy, Baby Bottle Pop. The band appeared in television commercials for the candy and in special videos and downloads available on the Baby Bottle Pop web site. The company also sponsored the band's 2007 "Invasion" tour, which featured songs from their first album from Hollywood Records, *Jonas Brothers.*

Unlike their debut album, *Jonas Brothers* was put together relatively quickly—in about a month's time. The CD was released on August 7, 2007, and debuted at No. 5 on the Billboard 200 list, with two hit singles—"Hold On" and "S.O.S."—leading the way. The album contains a mix of power pop and ballads that showed the band was just on the verge of stardom, according to many observers. *Los Angeles Times* writer Mikael Wood called the band "Green Day minus curse words," while a *USA Today* critic described their music as "pure power-pop ear candy." Another reviewer, Jay Lustig, commented in the *Newark Star-Ledger:* "Like a lot of their peers,

79

they have grown up amid the ubiquity of boy-band pop and emo-punk. And they see no reason not to combine the two. Their sound is glossy but not sappy, and their vocals can be sweet or snarling."

Writing about the hit song "S.O.S." in *Billboard* magazine, critic Chuck Taylor summed up the band's appeal like this: "With its manic faux-wave beat, storytelling lyric about a broken heart primed for healing, and ready-made teen idol vocals from 17-year-old Joe Jonas, the latter song's appeal is just opening the door for the phenom in store for the sibling threesome. These dudes have it all: versatility, youth, looks, and hooks. Truly a match made in pop heaven."

———— **"** ————

"Joseph just has this really cool, smooth rock voice,"

Nick said. "He really knows how to get the crowd going. Kevin is the one that holds us all together. Joseph and I are the singers and we take turns on keyboards and percussion, but Kevin mostly plays the guitar and that's the part of the group that we need—he's the glue that keeps it together."

———— **"** ————

Stage Presence

Two years after putting their act together, the Jonas Brothers are now confident and happy performing as a rock band. Their shows are high-energy events. "I'm pretty much stationary," Kevin said, "just singing and playing my guitar. But Joseph and Nick, they run and do a ton. They jump around all over the place. Sometimes, if someone in the front row isn't paying attention, Joseph will run over and tap her on the shoulder and just start singing in her face. . . . It's a way to get everyone involved."

Nick offered his analysis of the group's appeal: "Joseph just has this really cool, smooth rock voice. . . . He really knows how to get the crowd going. Kevin is the one that holds us all together. Joseph and I are the singers and we take turns on keyboards and percussion, but Kevin mostly plays the guitar and that's the part of the group that we need—he's the glue that keeps it together."

Thanks to their good looks, the boys do have some girls who follow them from show to show, but they aren't too comfortable with attention for their looks. "We wear rings on our fingers that are purity rings, so we stay pure until marriage," Joe pointed out. He also noted that their appeal isn't limited to girls. "Guys will always come up to us after a show and say, 'Dude—

Performing onstage at Six Flags—Magic Mountain.

you rock,' which is great." Above all, he said, "We want to be a good influence. . . . We want people to have a good time with our music."

While the brothers' Christian faith is not at the forefront of their lyrics, it is definitely an influence on their overall tone and is a vital part of their daily lives and their performances. Although their songs thus far haven't been particularly religious, Kevin has said that "we hope to break into the Christian market after we've had success in the pop market." Joe said that before every show, "We pray that the sound is fine, that we have the right energy." They call the last 45 minutes before show time "lockdown," and as Joe explained, "It's just us and no one comes in and no one goes out. It's a cool time to get focused and we just get psyched and really excited about the show."

Future Plans

The future for the Jonas Brothers looks very positive, as Disney continues to give the band strong support. A TV special, *Jonas Brothers in Concert*, premiered in late 2007. A series pilot has been filmed for a television show called "J.O.N.A.S.," an acronym for Junior Operatives Networking As

Spies. This comedy/spy series will feature their music as well as funny and exciting adventures involving their work as espionage agents. In addition, the band is slated to star in *Camp Rock,* a Disney Channel original musical movie that is planned for 2008.

The brothers are enjoying their growing success and continue to appreciate it on a daily basis. "We wake up every day and we freak out," admitted Joseph. "You can't wake up and say, 'Oh, another show in front of fans.' We don't take any of this for granted. It's such a blessing. It's seriously our dream come true."

> "We wake up every day and we freak out," admitted Joseph. "You can't wake up and say, 'Oh, another show in front of fans.' We don't take any of this for granted. It's such a blessing. It's seriously our dream come true."

HOME AND FAMILY

The Jonases still own their home in Wyckoff, but since the boys' career has taken off, the family has moved their home base to Los Angeles, California. "We're still New Jersey boys at heart," Nick commented.

The Jonas family is close-knit. One parent usually travels with the boys as they tour, and their tour manager is an uncle. Although their music has a punk sound, Nick says that on the whole, the boys are "good about not getting into trouble—we don't see the point." Their parents don't hesitate to discipline them, according to Nick. "They do not mind grounding us from our cell phones and TV—not me too much, because I'm a good kid—but Kevin and Joe get their cell phones grounded almost every day, just for being stupid, I guess, not taking out the trash or washing dishes."

The brothers are happy to perform together, because as family members, according to Nick, "You have a security that everything is going to be okay, even when you mess up." Kevin said that "It feels like the most natural thing we could be doing. When we write a song we get in a triangle. I start playing the chords that we've chosen over and over and then we'll keep going around in a circle until we have figured out the lyrics for our song." Joseph offered his perspective: "We're brothers so it's not like if we got upset at each other that we can be like, 'well I quit.' They're still my brothers. We love to do this and we know we're going to keep doing it for a very long time."

"I think we definitely fit in because we're different," Nick reflected. "We're not trying to be the next somebody. We're trying to be the Jonas brothers, and people enjoy that. There's nothing like us out there, and they appreciate our creativeness."

MEMORABLE EXPERIENCES

In November, 2005, Nick was diagnosed with Type 1 diabetes. Diabetes is a medical condition that occurs when the body does not produce enough insulin, a substance that is needed to convert sugar into energy the body can use. Before his diagnosis, Nick had the classic symptoms of the disorder: rapid weight loss (15 pounds in two weeks), extreme thirst (he was drinking 20 to 30 bottles of water a day), and extreme irritability. Nick was scared by his diagnosis, wondering if diabetes could even cause him to die.

He was admitted to the hospital to learn about his condition and how to control it. At first, he was required to give himself as many as ten insulin injections a day. Later, he switched to the use of an Omni Pod, a "smart pump" device that is worn as a patch on the skin. Controlled by a hand-held, wireless device that looks something like an iPod, the Omni Pod can monitor blood sugar levels and deliver the correct dosages of insulin automatically, without the need for injections.

——— *"* ———

"At first, I was worried that diabetes would keep me from performing and recording and doing everything a teenager likes to do, but, my career is really ramping up," Nick said. *"I want to let kids know that it doesn't have to be so hard. The most important thing is to never ever let yourself get down about having diabetes, because you can live a really great life as a kid with diabetes."*

——— *"* ———

Nick went public with his condition in March 2007, while playing at the Diabetes Research Institute's Carnival for a Cure, held in New York City. Asking for a show of hands from people in the audience who had diabetes, he then surprised the crowd by raising his own hand. "At first, I was worried that diabetes would keep me from performing and recording and doing everything a teenager likes to do, but, my career is really ramping up," Nick said. "I want to let kids know that it doesn't have to be so hard. The most important thing is to never ever let yourself get down about having diabetes, because you can live a really great life as a kid with diabetes."

FAVORITE MUSIC

The Jonas brothers enjoy a wide range of music, including Weird Al Yankovic, Backstreet Boys, My Chemical Romance, Stevie Wonder, Sham '69, the Ramones, Switchfoot, Coldplay, Fall Out Boy, Motion City Soundtrack, and Jack's Mannequin.

HOBBIES AND OTHER INTERESTS

When they aren't busy with music, the boys enjoy playing Xbox 360, basketball and other sports, and making movies.

SELECTED RECORDINGS

It's About Time, 2006
Zoey 101: Music Mix, 2006 (contributor)
Jonas Brothers, 2007
Meet the Robinsons, 2007 (soundtrack; contributor)

FURTHER READING

Periodicals

Billboard, Feb. 24, 2007, p.57; Nov. 3, 2007, p.53
Kansas City Star, Feb. 9, 2006
New Haven (CT) Register, Feb. 16, 2006
New York Times, June 18, 2006, p.11
Newark (NJ) Star-Ledger, Apr. 24, 2007, p.19
People, Aug. 27, 2007, p.79
Village Voice, May 3, 2006
Wall Street Journal, July 19, 2007

Online Articles

http://www.ym.com
    (YM.com, "Meet the Jonas Brothers," June 14, 2007)

ADDRESS

Jonas Brothers
Hollywood Records
500 South Buena Vista Street
Burbank, CA 91521

WORLD WIDE WEB SITES

http://www.jonasbrothers.com
http://www.kenphillipsgroup.com/Phillips/jonasbrothers.htm

Scott Niedermayer 1973-

Canadian Hockey Player with the Anaheim Ducks
All-Star Defenseman and 2007 Conn Smythe
Trophy Winner

BIRTH

Scott Niedermayer (pronounced *NEE dur MY ur*) was born
on August 31, 1973, in Edmonton, Alberta, Canada. His
mother, Carol, was a schoolteacher, and his father, Bob, was
a surgeon. Scott has one brother, Rob, who is 18 months
younger. Their parents divorced when the boys were both in
their teens.

YOUTH AND EDUCATION

Scott and his brother Rob were raised in Cranbrook, British Columbia, a town of about 20,000 people nestled on the western edge of the Canadian Rockies. Cranbrook is a community in which outdoor activities like skiing, fishing, and hockey are enormously popular, and the Niedermayer boys enthusiastically participated in these and other activities. Over time, however, hockey became their primary focus.

Carol Niedermayer provided valuable coaching to both of her sons during their youths. A power skating instructor, she was able to carve out free ice time at the local rink for her and her boys. During the school year, she regularly picked them up at lunch time, gave them skating lessons at the arena, then delivered them back to school before their classes resumed. These lessons gave Scott and Rob a valuable boost over other players their age. By the time they were 10 or 11 years old, they were known as two of the top young players in the region.

> *"They're good kids, but they were typical boys growing up," recalled Carol Niedermayer. "Believe me, they got into plenty of mischief."*

Scott and Rob shared a passion for hockey, but they still engaged in the usual brotherly quarrels. "They're good kids, but they were typical boys growing up," recalled Carol Niedermayer. "Believe me, they got into plenty of mischief." As the older brother, Scott had admitted that he did his share of picking on his smaller sibling when they were kids. But when Rob experienced a growth spur in his mid-teens, Scott sensibly curtailed his teasing. "He was a lot smaller until he was 14 or 15," he recalled. "Then we stopped fighting."

At age 15 Scott left home to play for a junior hockey team in nearby Kamloops. He spent the rest of his teen years tearing up the Western Hockey League (WHL) as a member of the Kamloops Blazers. Rob also joined a junior hockey club at age 15, but he played for a team in Medicine Hat. Both boys showed a lot of promise, but Scott was clearly the greater star of the two. In 1991 he helped lift Team Canada to a gold medal finish in the 1991 World Junior Hockey Championships. One year later, he led Kamloops to the WHL championship, earning league most valuable player honors in the process.

Niedermayer during his rookie season with the Devils, playing at Madison Square Garden in New York. Teammate Doug Brown is behind him.

CAREER HIGHLIGHTS

Niedermayer's exploits in the WHL caught the attention of scouts from all across the National Hockey League (NHL). In the 1991 NHL Draft, the New Jersey Devils selected him with the third overall pick. Niedermayer's lifelong dream of playing professional hockey was about to come true.

Joining the New Jersey Devils

During his first few seasons with the Devils, Niedermayer experienced both exciting triumphs and disappointing setbacks. He earned a spot on the NHL All-Rookie Team in 1992-93 as a defenseman, and the following year he played an important role as the team cruised to its best-ever regular season record. But the Devils continued to fall short in their efforts to reach the Stanley Cup Finals. In addition, Niedermayer became frustrated at times with the defensive philosophy of Head Coach Jacques Lemaire, a conservative coach who preached positioning and conservative play to his defensemen. Niedermayer understood Lemaire's philosophy, but he felt that it did not take full advantage of his fluid skating style and offensive skills.

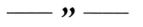

> *"I love the offensive part of the game—I like to rush, and I love to score. But Jacques' system has worked—you can't argue with that. We won the Cup. Someday I'll get the chance to play a more open style, but for now I'm happy here."*

In the 1994-95 season, though, Niedermayer and the Devils finally broke through to claim the franchise's first-ever Stanley Cup. After New Jersey swept the Detroit Red Wings in four games to claim the 1995 Cup, Niedermayer expressed satisfaction with his career and his progress as a player. "I love the offensive part of the game—I like to rush, and I love to score. But Jacques' system has worked—you can't argue with that. We won the Cup. Someday I'll get the chance to play a more open style, but for now I'm happy here."

Niedermayer continued to hone his game over the next several years, both in the NHL and in international competition. In 1996 he was named to Team Canada for the 1996 World Cup of Hockey. This prestigious event, which was known as the Canada Cup until the early 1990s, brings together the top hockey-playing nations around the globe. Canada advanced to the finals, but was relegated to the silver medal when it fell one goal short against the gold-medal winning United States.

On Top of the World

Back in the NHL, Niedermayer continued his steady ascent into the front ranks of league defensemen. In both 1996-97 and 1997-98, New Jersey allowed the fewest goals in the entire league, and Niedermayer's play was an important factor in this achievement. At the same time, the swift skater became increasingly known for his offensive production. In the 1997-98 season, for example, Niedermayer led the Devils in three offensive categories—assists (43), power-play goals (11), and power-play points (29). In recognition of his growing value on both ends of the rink, he was named an all-star for the first time in 1998.

The Devils won a number of division and conference titles during these years, but their quest for a second Stanley Cup went unfulfilled until the 1999-2000 season. Niedermayer led New Jersey's defensemen in scoring for the fifth straight campaign that year, and his steady play in the defensive zone was instrumental in getting the team back to the Finals. The Devils and Head Coach Larry Robinson then knocked off the Dallas Stars in six hard-fought games.

With the season behind him, Niedermayer celebrated his second Stanley Cup in an unusual fashion. According to NHL tradition, each player and coach on the winning team is permitted to keep the Cup for a 24-hour period during the offseason, before the trophy is returned to its regular home at the Hockey Hall of Fame in Toronto in Ontario, Canada. Most players and coaches take the Cup to their hometowns or other places that are important to them for parties with family and friends. Niedermayer, though, took the Cup with him and his family on a helicopter ride to the summit of Fisher Peak, one of the highest peaks in all of British Columbia. He then posed for a photo session for *Canadian Geographic* as his family looked on. His brother Ron joined the fun, but he kept his vow that he would not touch the trophy until he earned a championship himself.

A Family Affair

In 2001-02, the Devils limped to a disappointing third-place finish in the Atlantic Division and a first-round loss in the playoffs. The high point of the season for Niedermayer was actually a mid-season break so that NHL players could participate in the 2002 Winter Olympics in Salt Lake City, Utah. He was a member of the Team Canada squad that defeated the United States 5-2 to claim Olympic gold.

Niedermayer hoisting the Stanley Cup on the top of Fisher Peak, near his hometown of Cranbrook, British Columbia.

New Jersey rebounded from its shaky 2001-02 season one year later, thanks in large part to Niedermayer's steady defensive play and stellar special teams work. After claiming the Atlantic Division crown, the Devils cruised through the opening rounds of the playoffs to reach the Stanley Cup Finals once again. Their foe in the 2003 Stanley Cup championship was the Anaheim Ducks—the team for which Rob Niedermayer played.

The prospect of brothers playing on opposing teams for the first time in Stanley Cup history attracted plenty of attention. Carol Niedermayer further stirred the publicity pot when she admitted that she would be rooting for the Ducks since Rob had not yet won an NHL championship. Scott took the news in stride, assuring everyone that he understood his mother's perspective on the series.

As it turned out, Scott and his Devils teammates disappointed Carol Niedermayer by earning a third Stanley Cup in a tense and exciting seven-game series. Scott was thrilled to win the Cup once again, but he freely admitted afterward that he felt badly for his younger brother. "I was disappointed for him," he said. "To put that much time and sacrifice and commitment to get there . . . to be that close and all of a sudden nothing, it's a pretty devastating feeling."

— **"** —

"I was disappointed for him,"
Scott said. "To put that much
time and sacrifice and
commitment to get there . . .
to be that close and all of a
sudden nothing, it's a pretty
devastating feeling."

— **"** —

One month after their Stanley Cup showdown, the Niedermayer brothers flew to Prague, the capital city of the Czech Republic, to train with Team Canada for the upcoming 2004 World Ice Hockey Championships. The experience was a tremendous one for both men. Not only did Canada win the gold medal with a 5-3 victory over Sweden in the final, the tournament gave them a rare opportunity to play hockey together. "It was new for us," Rob said afterward. "It got us thinking that before both of us retired, we wanted to play on the same team together."

Moving to the Anaheim Ducks

Scott Niedermayer returned to the international stage with Team Canada in the fall of 2004, at the World Cup of Hockey. Once again his cool approach and graceful skating proved vital to the team's success. Anchored by the steady play of Niedermayer and other veteran stars, Team Canada beat the Czech Republic in the semifinals and then claimed the gold medal with a 3-2 victory over Finland in the finals.

Niedermayer returned to North America to prepare for the upcoming NHL season, but the entire 2004-05 season was cancelled due to a bitter labor dispute between players and team owners. In July 2005 the two sides finally agreed on a new long-term contract to get the NHL up and running

Niedermayer was happy to be able to play alongside his brother Rob on the Anaheim Ducks.

again. Niedermayer's contract with the Devils had expired during the dispute, however, making him a free agent for the upcoming season.

New Jersey wanted to re-sign their star defenseman, and several other NHL teams courted him as well. But his brother Rob's team, the Anaheim Ducks, offered him a four-year, $27 million contract. Given the chance to play side-by-side with his brother, Niedermayer quickly signed up.

As the 2005-06 NHL campaign got underway, Niedermayer knew that he had made the right decision. For one thing, he loved being united with his brother. "It's just little things," he explained. "You to go practice, he's there every day. On the road, maybe we got out for dinner. Not every day. But it's always there. We're competing together for our team, trying to help us win. It's a lot of fun. It's something we'll remember forever."

Making Waves

In addition, the Ducks coaching staff turned Niedermayer loose, giving him greater freedom to rush into the offensive zone. As a result, he tallied a career-best 63 points (13 goals and 50 assists) in 2005-06 without losing any of his effectiveness on the defensive end of the ice. The Ducks were thrilled with Niedermayer's instant impact on the team. "Ask anyone who works here, they will tell you they were amazed at how good Scotty was," said General Manager Brian Burke. "We knew he was a great player, but it isn't until you see him every day that you realize how much he dominates games. Then there is the side the public doesn't see—the quiet, effective leadership side."

Niedermayer and a core group of talented young players helped drive Anaheim deep into the 2005-06 playoffs. The Ducks knocked off the heavily favored Calgary Flames in seven games, then swept the Colorado Avalanche before being sidelined by the Edmonton Oilers in the Western Conference Finals.

Prior to the 2006 season, the Ducks signed star defenseman Chris Pronger, giving the club two of the finest defensive players in the entire NHL. Pronger's tough, intimidating presence made Anaheim even more formidable, but Niedermayer remained the undisputed team leader "A lot of the guys in this [locker] room look to Scotty for that leadership," said Ducks center Andy McDonald. "He has an even-keel outlook. He doesn't get too high or too low. That kind of attitude is contagious. You see it rubbing off on the younger guys." Ducks right wing Teemu Selanne voiced similar sentiments. "Everybody respects him so much. He's not the most vocal guy, but the way he leads by example and how he approaches things, it's just unbelievable."

Niedermayer loved being united with his brother on the Anaheim Ducks. "It's just little things," he explained. "You to go practice, he's there every day. On the road, maybe we got out for dinner. Not every day. But it's always there. We're competing together for our team, trying to help us win. It's a lot of fun. It's something we'll remember forever."

Head Coach Randy Carlyle also sang Niedermayer's praises. He noted that "a player of that caliber has the ability to play the huge minutes," but he indicated that the veteran defenseman's leadership qualities were even more important to the team. "I think the one thing you can say about Scott Niedermayer is he has a calming effect on your group. When things get a little hairy, and they always do at certain times, he has the ability to just slow down the tempo or speed up the tempo at the right time. . . . He's very unassuming in the way he handles himself. But I would say that the

No. 1 asset for him as a person is his ability to calm things down and calm people down in tense situations."

Winning another Stanley Cup

The Ducks roared out of the gate at the beginning of the 2006-07 season and never looked back. Anaheim posted the second-best regular season record in the Western Conference, in part because Niedermayer posted his best ever offensive season with 69 points (15 goals and 54 assists). In the playoffs, he seemed to provide a goal whenever the team needed it most. He scored a series-clinching double overtime goal over Vancouver in the second round of the playoffs. Then, in a pivotal Game Two conference final contest against the Detroit Red Wings, he once again scored an overtime game-winner. Three games later against the Wings, he scored a goal in the final minute of regulation to force overtime in a crucial 2-1 Anaheim victory.

> "A lot of the guys in this [locker] room look to Scotty for that leadership," said Ducks center Andy McDonald. "He has an even-keel outlook. He doesn't get too high or too low. That kind of attitude is contagious. You see it rubbing off on the younger guys."

Thanks in part to Niedermayer's heroics, Anaheim was able to slip past Detroit in six games to advance to the Stanley Cup Finals. The last obstacle to a Stanley Cup championship was the Ottawa Senators, the Eastern Conference champ. But the series proved to be a lopsided one, with the Ducks cruising to victory in five games. After Anaheim won Game Five by a 6-2 score to earn the franchise's first NHL championship, Niedermayer was the first Duck to hoist the Stanley Cup above his head and skate around the rink. When he was done celebrating, he handed the Cup over to his brother Rob, who then got to hold the Cup for the first time in his career. For his outstanding performance in the playoffs, Scott Niedermayer was named the series MVP, winning the Conn Smythe Trophy.

Anaheim's Stanley Cup triumph marked the first time since the 1982-83 season that brothers were on the same Cup-winning team. Since the formation of the NHL in 1918, 15 sets of brothers have shared the Stanley Cup. The most recent set was Brent and Duane Sutter of the 1983 New York Islanders.

Rob and Scott Niedermayer pose with Scott's sons,
Logan, Jackson, and Josh, after winning the 2007 Stanley Cup.

Afterwards, Scott said he treasures all four of his Stanley Cup championship teams. But he acknowledged that winning the fourth one with his brother had added significance for him. "It hits pretty hard right in the heart," Niedermayer declared. "Our names will be side-by-side forever, on the Cup, in the Hall of Fame. That's pretty special."

As the 2007-08 NHL season approached, many hockey observers speculated that Niedermayer might finally retire. After all, they said, how could he top winning a Stanley Cup with his brother? Niedermayer, however, had not made a final decision. "[My thinking about retiring] goes sort of in waves and ups and downs," he said. "It's a big decision.... I'm trying to give it the due respect and every consideration that every part of it deserves." Niedermayer was still undecided at the beginning of the season, so the Ducks placed him on the suspended list. He wasn't expected to decide until December 2007, over a month into the season. The Stanley Cup winners had a difficult start to the season, as Teemu Selanne was also on the suspended list pondering retirement, and several players were injured early on. Niedermayer was reported to feel that he should return and help out his teammates. At press time, his future plans remained uncertain.

> "It hits pretty hard right in the heart," Niedermayer declared. "Our names will be side-by-side forever, on the Cup, in the Hall of Fame. That's pretty special."

MARRIAGE AND FAMILY

Niedermayer and his wife Lisa have three sons, Logan, Jackson, and Joshua. The family divides its time between Anaheim and Niedermayer's hometown of Cranbrook, British Columbia.

HOBBIES AND OTHER INTERESTS

The Niedermayer brothers run a youth hockey camp in Cranbrook every summer.

HONORS AND AWARDS

Scholastic Player of the Year (Canadian Major Junior League): 1990-91
World Junior Championships: 1991, gold medal
Memorial Cup: 1992, gold medal

Stafford Smythe Memorial Trophy (Western Hockey League): 1991-92
NHL All-Rookie Team: 1992-93
World Cup of Hockey: 1996, silver medal; 2004, gold medal
NHL All-Star Team: 1997-98, 2000-01, 2003-04
Olympic Men's Hockey: 2002, gold medal
Norris Trophy (NHL Defensive Player of the Year): 2003-04
NHL First All-Star Team: 2003-04, 2006-07
World Ice Hockey Championships: 2004, gold medal
Mark Messier Leadership Award: 2006
Conn Smythe Trophy (NHL Playoffs Most Valuable Player): 2007

FURTHER READING

Periodicals

Canadian Geographic, Nov. 2000, p.23
Los Angeles Times, Sep. 1, 2005, p.D1; July 2, 2007, p.D1
New York Times, Feb. 2, 1998, p.C3; May 26, 2003, p.D1; Aug. 5, 2005, p.D7;
    Dec. 15, 2005, p.D6
Newark (NJ) Star-Ledger, May 28, 2007, p.37
Orange County (CA) Register, Apr. 13, 2006, SPORTS; June 6, 2007, p.C1
San Diego Union-Tribune, June 8, 2003, p.C8
Sports Illustrated, Jan. 8, 1996, p.46; Oct. 3, 2005, p.77; June 18, 2007, p.50
Sports Illustrated for Kids, Aug. 2007, p. 11
USA Today, June 2, 2003, p.C3; June 7, 2007, p.C10

ADDRESS

Scott Niedermayer
Anaheim Ducks
2695 East Katella Avenue
Anaheim, CA 92806

WORLD WIDE WEB SITES

http://ducks.nhl.com
http://www.nhl.com
http://www.nhlpa.com

Masi Oka 1974-

Japanese-American Actor and Special Effects Artist
Star of the Hit TV Show "Heroes"
Creator of Special Visual Effects for Movies including
The Perfect Storm, Star Wars: Episodes I, II, and *III,* and
Pirates of the Caribbean: Dead Man's Chest

BIRTH

Masayori (Masi) Oka was born on December 27, 1974, in
Tokyo, Japan. His parents divorced when he was only one
month old, and he never met his father. He was raised by his
mother, Setsuko Oka. He has no siblings.

YOUTH

In 1980, when Oka was six years old, he and his mother moved from Japan to Los Angeles, California. One of his earliest memories of being in the United States was his first trip to a pizzeria. he was eager to try what he thought was typical American food. "I had never had pizza before, and I was like, 'I'm in America, must get pizza!'" Oka was so excited that he didn't pay attention to where he was going in the restaurant. As he ran to a table, he bumped into a sharp corner and cut himself so badly that he needed stitches. When he and his mother got home from the hospital emergency room, Oka finally got his pizza. His mother had saved the pizza he ordered at the restaurant—one slice of cheese pizza and one slice of pepperoni.

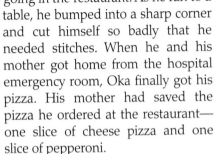

Oka values his heritage and is proud of being Japanese, but he is also grateful to his mother for making the decision to move to the United States. "Coming to America alone to raise a kid, she gave up everything for me. I owe her a lot."

Oka has lived in the U.S. for most of his life, but he has kept his Japanese citizenship. While he was growing up, he stayed connected to Japanese culture by reading Japanese anime and manga comic books, particularly the *Dragonball* series. His grandmother regularly sent him videotapes of everyday life in Japan, and Oka attended Japanese language school on weekends. Oka values his heritage and is proud of being Japanese, but he is also grateful to his mother for making the decision to move to the United States. "Coming to America alone to raise a kid, she gave up everything for me. I owe her a lot."

EDUCATION

As a child in Japan, Oka had performed very well on an intelligence test and he had been given a high Intelligence Quotient (IQ) score. An IQ score is a number intended to represent a person's mental abilities compared to others of the same age. Generally, a person with a high IQ score is thought to be smarter than the average person. The test is often used to predict a person's ability to learn, to do well in school, or to develop special talents. Some have felt that relying on a single test to predict a person's future is too limiting, and the accuracy and fairness of IQ tests are now questioned by some educators.

Oka's IQ has been reported as 180, which is considered genius. Because of his high IQ score, his mother decided to move to the United States so that he could go to American schools. She believed that in the U.S. he would get a more personalized education that would help to bring out any special talents he might have. Oka explained that when he was young, schools in Japan did not provide opportunities for individual students to excel. "So my mother made a conscious choice that we're going to go to America where you can go to a school where they're going to let your scientific skills, your mathematical skills, blossom. That's why she actually took that trip and made that jump to come to America."

Although the media has focused attention on his high IQ score, Oka himself prefers to downplay his reported intelligence. He has said in numerous interviews that he wished his IQ score had not become a topic for public discussion. "I'm just book smart. But definitely not street smart. . . . I would rather kind of lower everyone's expectations. I'd rather be kind of dumb and exceed peoples' expectations rather than . . . raise the bar and not be able to meet it."

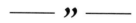

"I'm just book smart. But definitely not street smart. . . . I would rather kind of lower everyone's expectations. I'd rather be kind of dumb and exceed peoples' expectations rather than . . . raise the bar and not be able to meet it."

Oka attended Harvard Westlake School in Los Angeles, an independent college preparatory school for grades 7-12. His favorite subjects in school were those that involved computers. "I've been programming computers since elementary school, where they taught us, and I stuck with computer science through high school and college. . . . I've always loved problem-solving and the computers kind of help you do that." Oka graduated from high school in 1992. After graduation, he worked at the 1992 Summer Olympics in Barcelona, Spain, as an English, Japanese, and Spanish translator.

Oka then attended Brown University in Providence, Rhode Island. He always knew that he wanted to study computer programming, but he was also interested in acting. Not wanting to limit himself to only one area of study, Oka chose to attend Brown instead of a more technical university so that he could get a well-rounded education. "I thought, 'You know what, college is a place where I need to grow as a human being.' I wanted to learn more about myself and get a social education, not just an academic one. I could always go to Harvard or MIT for graduate school." In 1997, Oka received a Bachelor of Science (BS) degree in computer science and mathematics with a minor in theater arts from Brown University.

CAREER HIGHLIGHTS

After college, Oka went to work for Industrial Light & Magic (ILM), the visual effects studio founded by filmmaker George Lucas, who also created the *Star Wars* movies. "ILM offered me an entry-level position . . . but they refused to fly me out for the job interview. Fortunately, Microsoft also was interested in hiring me and they flew me out to Seattle, then down to San Francisco and back to Providence." Oka was offered a job at Microsoft, but took a job at ILM instead because the position there would allow him to combine his love of computers with his interest in movies and acting.

Pioneering Special Effects

Oka became a digital artist and technical director at ILM. His work there allowed him to write computer programs that were used to create special effects for many popular movies. He contributed to important scenes in many films, including all of the *Star Wars* prequels, *Episode I—The Phantom Menace* (1999), *Episode II—Attack of the Clones* (2002), and *Episode III— Revenge of the Sith* (2006), as well as *The Perfect Storm* (2000), *Terminator 3: Rise of the Machines* (2003), *Hulk* (2003), *War of the Worlds* (2005), and *Pirates of the Caribbean: Dead Man's Chest* (2006). Many of Oka's computer programs supported the creation of new and unique special effects, allowing ILM's artists to expand the range of possibilities for the digital movie effects known as CG (computer graphics).

One of the first large projects that Oka worked on was the 1999 *Star Wars* prequel *Episode I—The Phantom Menace.* For this movie, he created new computer software that allowed digital artists to produce any kind of solid-material explosion that they wanted. "With *Star Wars* there was a whole explosion effect of Obi Wan Kenobi's chase sequence through the asteroids and they wanted a way to destroy the asteroids. So they came up with different shots, to blow up the asteroid in a million pieces, but they didn't have the software. . . . I'd come up with software, and write the tools to create that explosion and I would teach it to the artists and they would adjust it and tweak it to get the image they wanted."

Oka's reputation as a talented programmer grew because of his cutting-edge CG work for the 2000 movie *The Perfect Storm.* Telling the dramatic story of a fishing boat stranded in the Atlantic Ocean during a severe storm, the movie presented many special effects challenges. At that time,

Oka designed software to create special effects for many popular movies, including the storm scenes in The Perfect Storm.

creating realistic simulated water effects was one of the most difficult things to do with computer graphics. As part of the largest ILM team ever assembled for a non-science-fiction movie, Oka designed innovative new software that revolutionized the creation of computerized water effects. His work allowed ILM's digital artists to create the impressive ocean storm scenes that were the focal point of the movie.

—————— " ——————

"With Star Wars there was a whole explosion effect of Obi Wan Kenobi's chase sequence through the asteroids. . . . They came up with different shots, to blow up the asteroid in a million pieces, but they didn't have the software. . . . I'd come up with software, and write the tools to create that explosion and I would teach it to the artists and they would adjust it and tweak it to get the image they wanted."

—————— " ——————

Although the movie itself received mixed reviews, critics and film industry professionals praised *The Perfect Storm* for its breakthrough special effects technology. The movie was nominated for many awards, including an Academy Award for Best Effects/Best Visual Effects and a Saturn Award for Best Special Effects from the Academy of Science Fiction, Fantasy & Horror Films. All of the water effects in *The Perfect Storm* were produced using computer programs that Oka wrote. His programs have been used in many movies since then, including *Pirates of the Caribbean: Dead Man's Chest* (2006).

"For *Pirates of the Caribbean [Dead Man's Chest]* they used a lot of the water stuff I wrote for *The Perfect Storm,*" Oka said. "You know, lots of particles of water stuff, and their interactions. Most of the stuff in *Pirates* was Davey Jones and the water dripping off him, and being able to control the drip. So they can say at this frame I want four drips, or streams down his face, and we could do that. . . . Of course, you can't time that in the practical world. But with CG you can do all that."

Taking a Chance on Acting

After finishing work on *The Perfect Storm*, Oka needed a break from special effects. While he thoroughly enjoyed his job at ILM, he still wanted to be an actor. By 2001, he had already become a member of the Screen Actors Guild by appearing in various technical training films in the San Francisco area. Oka felt it was time to pursue larger roles, and so he decided to move to Los Angeles to look for parts in television and movies.

ILM allowed Oka to transfer temporarily to their office in Los Angeles on one condition: he had to get a part in either a movie or a television series within one year. If he could not find any acting jobs, he would have to return to his job in San Francisco or leave ILM. Oka signed a contract with ILM agreeing to these terms, and he moved to Los Angeles. "I only gave myself a year to make it, which of course is very naïve," he recalled. "Because anyone who's trying to pursue a career in the entertainment industry knows that it's a marathon, not a sprint. But I made a bet with ILM that was signed into my contract, that if I didn't get a recurring role in a pilot or a supporting role in a film during my first year in L.A., then I'd go back to San Francisco full time."

Within a short time, Oka landed a part in the pilot episode of a television series called "Straight White Male." The show was never aired on television, but his role in the pilot meant that he'd fulfilled his contract and could stay in Los Angeles. While Oka continued to work on various projects for ILM, he also performed improvisational comedy and managed to get small roles in movies and television shows. He appeared in episodes of the TV shows "Without A Trace," "Sabrina the Teenage Witch," "Reba," "Reno 911!," "Gilmore Girls," "Dharma & Greg," and "Punk'd," and he also appeared in small parts in the movies *Austin Powers: Goldmember, Legally Blonde 2,* and *Along Came Polly.* In his first recurring role in a television series, Oka played Franklyn the lab technician on "Scrubs" (2002-2004). Throughout this time, he also worked with several improvisation groups such as Second City, ImprovOlympics, TheatreSports, and The Groundlings.

Oka realized that finding so many roles so quickly is unusual for an aspiring actor. He believed that being Japanese helped him get more acting

———— **"** ————

"To be honest . . . it's much easier to break into roles. There's less competition . . . and the producers are more open to changing smaller, one-line roles into bigger roles," he explained. "The hard part is to sustain a career. How many visible Asian actors are out there? When you compare the number to the total population it's significantly lower."

———— **"** ————

Oka in season one of "Heroes," backstage in Las Vegas among the show girls.

work during his first few years in Los Angeles. "To be honest . . . it's much easier to break into roles. There's less competition . . . and the producers are more open to changing smaller, one-line roles into bigger roles," he explained. "The hard part is to sustain a career. How many visible Asian actors are out there? When you compare the number to the total population it's significantly lower."

"Heroes"

Oka contined to get small roles regularly, but by 2005 he was almost ready to give up hope of landing larger parts. He decided to try one last season of auditions for TV series pilots. If he wasn't offered any substantial acting work, he intended to focus on screenwriting and producing his ideas for TV shows and movies while continuing to work for ILM.

The first role that Oka auditioned for that year was one that he completely identified with. The character was a Japanese computer programmer who loved comic books, and the show's producers were looking for a Japanese-speaking Asian actor with comedy experience. The role seemed almost as if it had been created especially for Oka, and he won the part of Hiro Nakamura in the pilot episode of a television show called "Heroes."

"Heroes" was not only Oka's first pilot to be made into a television series, it was an instant hit and became the most popular new television show of 2006. The comic-book style series follows the adventures of a group of people as they each discover that they have extraordinary and mysterious superpowers. Hiro is one of several characters whose intersecting stories gradually reveal that they must all work together to save the world. In its first broadcast season, the show regularly attracted more than 15 million viewers each week, placing it consistently among the top 20 most-watched programs.

On "Heroes," Oka plays Hiro Nakamura, an office worker who loves comics and videogames and who suddenly realizes that he has the ability to manipulate time and space through sheer will power. Hiro can stop time, travel instantly to another place, and travel back and forth through time to visit the past or the future. Because of his love of comic books and superheroes, Hiro is excited to have these powers and knows exactly what he wants to do with them. Unlike the other "Heroes" characters, Hiro enjoys being a superhero. The character was an afterthought that was added to the pilot at the last minute after it was observed that none of the other characters were happy to be superheroes.

Hiro was originally intended to simply be one of many characters on the show. Everyone, including Oka, was surprised when Hiro became the breakout star of the series. "He was comedic relief and he embraced being a superhero. But from my perspective, he was a foreign character who doesn't speak any English and he's a geek. I wasn't sure how much the audience would be able to relate to him." In attempting to explain his character's wide appeal, Oka said, "He's basically a wide-eyed kid full of wonder. He's the kind of person so many of us want to be, but we lose much of that wonder as we grow up and grapple with societal pressures."

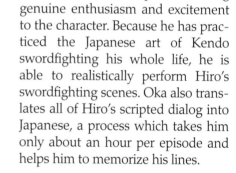

"He was comedic relief and he embraced being a superhero," Oka said about his character, Hiro. "But from my perspective, he was a foreign character who doesn't speak any English and he's a geek. I wasn't sure how much the audience would be able to relate to him."

Oka puts a lot of himself into his portrayal of Hiro, and the "Heroes" writers have also included his personality and some of his talents in the role. Oka's lifelong love of science fiction, anime, and comics helps him to bring genuine enthusiasm and excitement to the character. Because he has practiced the Japanese art of Kendo swordfighting his whole life, he is able to realistically perform Hiro's swordfighting scenes. Oka also translates all of Hiro's scripted dialog into Japanese, a process which takes him only about an hour per episode and helps him to memorize his lines.

Critics have praised Oka's Hiro as a refreshing, childlike character who is full of joy and spirit. *Wired* magazine called his portrayal of Hiro endearing and said that Hiro's geekiness gives him an edge in popularity over the other characters on the show. *Wired* also praised his acting, saying, "In an ensemble cast that features solid acting all around, Oka steals the show every time he's on the screen." An *Entertainment Weekly* critic applauded his "gleeful cheer" in the role of Hiro and credited Oka for keeping fans riveted to the show. A reviewer writing for msnbc.com called Oka's portrayal of Hiro "brilliantly crafted" and stated that "Masi Oka is so cool, he should get an award just for being Masi Oka."

Oka was nominated for many awards in 2007 for his role on "Heroes," including a Golden Globe Award for Best Performance by an Actor in a Supporting Role in a Series, Mini-Series or Motion Picture Made for Television; an Emmy Award for Outstanding Supporting Actor in a Drama Series; and a Teen Choice Award. He received a 2007 Saturn Award for Best Supporting Actor in a Television Program from the Academy of Science Fiction,

*Scenes from "Heroes,"
seasons one and two.*

Fantasy & Horror Films. He also won a 2007 Future Classic Award from TV Land and a 2007 Asian Excellence Award for Outstanding Actor in Television from AZN Television. Oka was also named one of *Wired* magazine's Rave Award winners in 2007.

——— " ———

"Laughter is kind of a symbolism of peace. It's easy to cry, but it's so hard to laugh. . . . Love and laughter are universal. Romantic comedies are my specialty, because they transcend the beliefs you have, your religion, your ethnicity, your cultural background. That's a direction I would love to go."

——— " ———

Looking to the Future

Oka's success on "Heroes" has resulted in new opportunities in movies. In 2007, he will appear in the *Get Smart* movies as well as the table-tennis themed comedy *Balls of Fury*. In addition to acting, Oka sees his career eventually growing to include directing, particularly comedies. "Laughter is kind of a symbolism of peace. It's easy to cry, but it's so hard to laugh. . . . Love and laughter are universal. Romantic comedies are my specialty, because they transcend the beliefs you have, your religion, your ethnicity, your cultural background. That's a direction I would love to go."

His current filming schedule keeps him very busy, but Oka continues to work part-time for ILM as a consultant. He is only able to work on ILM projects for the equivalent of about three days each week. Working for ILM allows Oka to achieve the goals he set as a child, when he was determined to embrace all of his interests and be successful in more than one kind of job. As he explained, "I always dreamed of winning two Oscars—one technical, one creative."

Oka has also remained philosophical about being categorized by the media as a nerdy geek. "Being a geek is a great thing. I think we're all geeks. Being a geek means you're passionate about something and that defines your uniqueness. I would rather be passionate about something than be apathetic about everything."

HOME AND FAMILY

Oka is single and lives in Los Angeles. He still has a close relationship with his mother, who he says is his real-life superhero. "Anyone who raises a child as a single mother is a hero." He credits her support for his success both behind the scenes and in front of the camera. "She's told me, 'Do what you want to do. Live a life that you don't regret. No matter what happens, make sure that's what you want to do. Just be happy with it and don't have regrets.'"

HOBBIES AND OTHER INTERESTS

Oka speaks English, Japanese, and Spanish. His hobbies include practicing the Kendo style of Japanese swordfighting, playing video games, playing the piano, and singing. He enjoys reading Japanese manga comics, especially those of his favorite author Naoki Urasawa. Oka also writes romantic comedy screenplays. His favorite romantic comedies are *When Harry Met Sally, The Princess Bride, Serendipity,* and *Notting Hill.*

SELECTED CREDITS

Acting

"Scrubs," 2002-04 (TV series)
"Heroes," 2006- (TV series)

Special Effects

Star Wars: Episode I—The Phantom Menace, 1999 (visual effects producer, technical support worker)
The Perfect Storm, 2000 (digital artist)
Star Wars: Episode II—Attack of the Clones, 2002 (digital effects artist)
Hulk, 2003 (technical director)
Terminator 3: Rise of the Machines, 2003 (computer graphics artist)
Star Wars: Episode III—Revenge of the Sith, 2005 (digital artist)
War of the Worlds, 2005 (digital artist)
Pirates of the Caribbean: Dead Man's Chest, 2006 (digital artist)

Writing

Chester's Big Night, 2004 (short film screenplay)

HONORS AND AWARDS

Saturn Award (Academy of Science Fiction, Fantasy & Horror Films, USA): 2007, Best Supporting Actor in a Television Program, for "Heroes"
Future Classic Award (TV Land Awards): 2007, for "Heroes"
AZN Asian Excellence Award (AZN Television): 2007, Outstanding Actor—Television, for "Heroes"
Rave Award (*Wired* magazine): 2007, for "Heroes"

FURTHER READING

Books

Contemporary Theatre, Film, and Television, 2007

Periodicals

Boston Herald, May 7, 2007, p.031
Entertainment Weekly, Nov. 10, 2006, p.30; May 11, 2007, p.H17
Los Angeles Times, Oct. 29, 2006, p.E20
New York Times, Dec. 4, 2006, p.E3
San Francisco Chronicle, Apr. 23, 2007, p.C1
Seattle Times, May 14, 2007
USA Today, Nov. 19, 2006
Wired, Oct. 2006; May 2007, p.130

Online Articles

http://www.comic-con.org/cci/cci07prog_oka.shtml
  (Comic-Con 2007, "Extended Interview with Masi Oka," undated)
http://www.ifmagazine.com/feature.asp?article=2001
  (iF Magazine, "Exclusive Interview: Heroes Star Masi Oka Looks to the
  Future," Apr. 2, 2007)
http://www.msnbc.msn.com/id/16756741
  (MSNBC.com, "Super Hero: Japanese Nerd Is Hit of 'Heroes,'" Apr. 26, 2007)
http://www.mtv.com/ontv/dyn/trl/interviews.jhtml?interviewId=1560069
  (MTV.com, "TRL Interview: Masi Oka," undated)
http://www.wired.com/entertainment/hollywood/news/2007/04/magkring
  (Wired.com, "Behind the Scenes With 'Heroes' Creator Tim Kring and
  'Hiro' Masi Oka, Apr. 23, 2007)
http://www.wired.com/culture/lifestyle/news/2006/10/71984
  (Wired.com, "Masi Oka: Coder, Actor, Hero," Oct. 25, 2006)

Online Databases

Biography Resource Center Online, 2007, article from *Contemporary Theatre,
Film, and Televison,* 2007

ADDRESS

Masi Oka
"Heroes," NBC
30 Rockefeller Plaza
New York, NY 10112

WORLD WIDE WEB SITE

http://www.nbc.com/Heroes/bios/hiro.shtml

Morgan Pressel 1988-

American Professional Golfer
Youngest Woman Ever to Win a Major
Golf Championship

BIRTH

Morgan Pressel was born in Tampa, Florida, on May 23, 1988, the oldest child of Mike and Kathy (Krickstein) Pressel. Her parents owned a real estate business, and her mother was also a professional tennis coach. Pressel has a younger sister, Madison, and a younger brother, Mitchell. Both siblings are following their sister onto the junior golf circuit.

YOUTH

Pressel was born into a very athletic family. Her father played hockey in high school, while her mother won a Big Ten title in tennis at the University of Michigan. Her uncle, Aaron Krickstein, was only 16 when he became the youngest man ever to win a Grand Prix Championship on the Association of Tennis Professionals (ATP) Circuit. He was also the youngest to earn a top 20 world ranking. Pressel showed athletic talent at a young age, able to turn cartwheels at age two. She tried tennis, but her grandfather, Herb Krickstein, felt she wasn't quick enough to become an elite player. He did notice she had great hand-eye coordination, and at age eight he took her to the driving range. After seeing her natural golf swing, Pressel recalled, "he said, 'that's it, no more tennis.'"

Her parents left Morgan's training up to "Papa" Krickstein, a retired doctor who had experience managing his own kids to athletic success. He enlisted Martin Hall, who had worked with golf greats like Jack Nicklaus, to coach his granddaughter's swing. She practiced regularly, both at home in Florida and summers at her grandparents' home in Michigan. By age 11, Pressel had broken par for an 18-hole course, and by age 12, she was competing against adults—and beating them—in organized tournaments.

—— " ——

Pressel was only 15 when her mother died in 2003. "I grew up in a hurry," she recalled. "I've been through a lot. It was the toughest time in my life, and I miss her every day. I know my mother is always with me. She pops into my mind all the time."

—— " ——

Pressel was finding increasing success in golf, but athletics weren't the defining experience of her teen years. Her mother was diagnosed with breast cancer when Morgan was just 11. Despite going through surgery and chemotherapy, Kathy Pressel was able to support her daughter by attending tournaments. "She was always telling me to be dedicated and determined and competitive, because she was very competitive herself," Morgan remembered. Kathy Pressel fought hard, but her cancer recurred. She died in September 2003 at the age of 43. Morgan was only 15, and the loss devastated her. "I grew up in a hurry," she recalled. "I've been through a lot. It was the toughest time in my life, and I miss her every day. I know my mother is always with me. She pops into my mind all the time." Her mother's fighting spirit would serve as an inspiration to the young golfer.

GOLF SCORING

Golf scoring can be complicated to learn. Players keep track of how many "strokes" it takes them to hit the ball from the tee to the cup; the fewer strokes, the better. "Par" refers to the standard number of strokes it should take a player to complete each hole. For example, most golf courses include short holes, which are usually designated as "par 3," as well as longer holes, which are designated as "par 5." On a regulation, 18-hole golf course, par for all holes will add up to 72. Depending on the number of strokes taken on a given hole, a player can shoot par, a birdie (one under par), an eagle (two under par), a bogey (one over par), a double bogey (two over par), etc.

On the professional golf circuit, most tournaments take place over four days. Each day, all the players shoot one "round" of 18 holes. After the first two rounds, they often cut the field to the top 60 or 70 golfers (players either "make" or "miss the cut"). After all four rounds, the scores are totaled and the player with the lowest score wins the tournament. This format is called "stroke play." There are many tournaments on the women's professional golf tour, but the most prestigious are the four major or "Grand Slam" events: the British Open, the Kraft Nabisco Championship, the U.S. Women's Open, and the McDonald's LPGA Championship.

Many amateur tournaments and team tournaments (like the Solheim Cup) use a different scoring system, called "match play." In this system, golfers play one-on-one over 18 holes. Whoever takes the fewest strokes on a hole scores a single point; if the two golfers tie they split the point. They keep a running tally of holes; if Player A has won 5 holes and Player B has won 3 holes, Player A is considered "2 up." A match can end before 18 holes if one player mathematically eliminates the other. In this case, the final score is listed as two numbers: the first indicating how many up the winner was, the second showing how many holes were left over. The highest winning score in match play is thus "10-and-8," meaning the winner won the first 10 holes, so they did not need to play the last eight. If a round of 18 holes ends in a tie, the match goes to "sudden death" on extra holes—meaning that the first player to win a hole wins the match.

EDUCATION

Pressel attended St. Andrew's High School of Boca Raton, Florida. As a freshman, she placed second in the state golf finals; her last three years she won the state competition, setting records for both one-day and total scores. Her low scores also helped her team to state championships in 2002 and 2003. She graduated from St. Andrew's in 2006, earning a 3.9 grade point average with a schedule that included Advanced Placement classes. She scored well enough on the SAT (including 790 out of 800 on the math portion) to qualify for Duke University, which offered her a golf scholarship. She decided to forego college, however, to begin her career as a professional golfer.

CAREER HIGHLIGHTS

Enjoying a Brilliant Amateur Career

Pressel first garnered national attention for her golf game when she was only 12 years old. In 2001 she won a qualifying tournament for the U.S. Women's Open by shooting two under par, setting a record (later broken) as the youngest player ever to qualify for an LPGA event. At the Open (one of golf's four major championships), she played two rounds of 77 and missed the cut to play the final two rounds. Still, it was a respectable performance for someone so young—better than 19 pros scored that year—and it brought her national media attention. "I had so much fun that week, I knew I wanted to be a professional golfer," Pressel remembered. The competition "was a wakeup call, too," she added. "I saw how good these players were, how much I needed to improve, but I knew this is where I wanted to be every week."

Although Pressel gained attention by qualifying for professional tournaments at such a young age, she felt she could best develop her skills by competing in amateur events. She entered tournaments sponsored by the American Junior Golf Association (AJGA); by playing against golfers her own age, she learned to hone her game under pressure. Pressel also increased her practice time, devoting hours after school and on weekends to improving her game. In 2002 she participated in the PING Junior Solheim Cup, a team match-play competition between the top 12 girl golfers from the U.S. and Europe. She went undefeated in her matches to help the U.S. win the Cup. She also had at least three top-20 finishes at AJGA events that year, including a third-place tie at the Thunderbird International Junior.

In 2003 Pressel qualified for the U.S. Women's Open again. This time she made the cut and finished 52nd with an average of 76. She earned a fourth-place finish in the Rolex Girls Junior Championship and had a 12-stroke victory at the Buick Junior Open. She was again named to the PING Junior Solheim Cup team, but was unable to travel to Europe with the team because of her mother's illness, which also forced her to pull out of three tournaments that summer. Despite her up-and-down year, Pressel earned her first appearance on the Junior All-American First Team in 2003. After her mother's death, she found some solace on the golf course and in the knowledge that her mother would have wanted her to keep pursuing her dream.

In 2004, Pressel began achieving more consistent results in her tournaments. She tied for second at the Rolex Girls Junior Championship and tied for fourth at McDonald's Betsy Rawls Girls Championship. She also began a phe-

Pressel at age 12, when she qualified for the 2002 Women's Open Tournament. She was the youngest player ever to qualify for an LPGA event.

nomenal run of victories in AJGA invitational events, winning the Rolex Tournament of Champions in July; the Polo Golf Junior Classic in November; the Thunderbird International Junior in May 2005; the Rolex Girls Junior Championship in June 2005; and finally the McDonald's Betsy Rawls Girls Championship in July 2005. This accomplishment made her one of only two players to ever win the "Career AJGA Slam." She also helped the U.S. to another victory at the 2005 PING Junior Solheim Cup. Overall, she won 11 AJGA tournaments, including all five she entered in 2005. She set a record for largest margin of victory (16 strokes) in an AJGA tournament and was named AJGA Player of the Year in 2005.

Besides dominating AJGA events, Pressel was also having success in adult events, both amateur and professional. By early 2005 she was the nation's number one-ranked female amateur. She won the 2004 North and South Women's Amateur Golf Championship (their youngest champion ever) and the 2005 Women's Amateur Golf Championship—the latter by a dominating score of 9-and-8. Most impressive, she was the runner-up at the 2005 U.S. Women's Open. Going into the last hole, she was tied for the lead with Birdie Kim—until Kim hit a phenomenal shot out of a sand bunker and scored a birdie. "When her shot went in, it felt like someone smacking me on the head with a two-by-four," Pressel recalled. "Oh, no, somebody pinch me. That didn't just happen. I knew how tough it was to make birdie on that hole and that I'd probably just lost. But I gave it my best shot."

> ———— **"** ————
>
> *At the 2005 U.S. Women's Open, Pressel was tied for the lead with Birdie Kim on the last hole—until Kim hit a phenomenal shot out of a sand bunker and scored a birdie. "When her shot went in, it felt like someone smacking me on the head with a two-by-four," Pressel recalled. "Oh, no, somebody pinch me. That didn't just happen. I knew how tough it was to make birdie on that hole and that I'd probably just lost. But I gave it my best shot."*
>
> ———— **"** ————

During 2005 Pressel competed in seven LPGA events, making all seven cuts and never finishing below 25th place. She capped off her amateur career by winning the 2006 Nancy Lopez Award as the year's outstanding female amateur golfer. "I got a little taste of winning, and I want a whole lot more," Pressel stated of her amateur career. "AJGA golf was a great experience for me. I made a lot of friends, and I played well, and I competed against the toughest fields in junior golf for four years."

Turning Pro at 17

With her success on both the amateur and LPGA levels, Pressel decided she was ready to turn professional. LPGA rules state that a player must be 18 to apply for membership, but those between the ages of 15 and 18 can ask for an exception to the rule. She asked for, and was granted, permission to try to qualify for the LPGA tour. She attended LPGA "Qualifying School"—a five-round competition—and tied for sixth. This earned her "exempt" status for future LPGA events, meaning she could bypass qualifying. Based on this finish, she asked the LPGA to allow her to join the tour at the beginning of 2006, instead of having to wait for her birthday at the end of May. When the tour granted her request, Pressel called it "a dream come true."

Pressel reacts to a missed birdie putt during the 2005 U.S. Women's Open.

Although she was now competing as a professional, Pressel didn't try to change her game. "I don't think it's going to be that much different, I'm still out there trying to win tournaments and play my best," she said. "The only thing that has changed is the level of competition and hopefully my ability." The young golfer made the most of her new status on the LPGA tour. She earned nine top-10 finishes in 2006, including a third place at the Longs Drugs Challenge and three fifth-place ties. She competed in all the major tournaments, including her first McDonald's LPGA and British Open Championships; her best finish was a tie for 13th at the Kraft Nabisco Championship. In the 2006 season, she finished third in the rookie of the year race, with total winnings of $465,685. At the end of the year she was in 21st place in the Rolex Women's World Golf Rankings, and she was selected for the 16-member Team International for the Lexus Cup.

Although this was a promising start for a pro golfer, Pressel wasn't satisfied. "I didn't play as well as I would have liked," she later observed. So to get ready for 2007, "I worked really hard in the off season, worked hard in the gym, worked hard on my swing with my coach, Martin Hall, and I came out a little bit more prepared to play well this year. And I got a lot of experience last year. And I was certainly ready to compete and ready to win." She began the 2007 season with some promising performances. She tied for fourth at the SBS Open at Turtle Bay; the following week she tied for third at the Fields Open in Hawaii.

——— " ———

"I love to compete," Pressel noted. *"I love the search for perfection. I'm constantly refining things, trying to be as perfect a player as I can be."*

——— " ———

Entering the first major tournament of the 2007 season, the Kraft Nabisco Championship at Mission Hills Country Club in Rancho Mirage, California, Pressel had the same confidence and high hopes she has brought to all her tournaments. She played most of the tournament behind the leaders, starting the final round of 18 four strokes behind. But Pressel played the last 24 holes of the tournament without a single bogey, finishing three under par overall. Then she had to wait for the last golfers to finish their rounds. As she watched, the leader bogeyed four holes in a row and then missed a birdie on 18, leaving Pressel alone in the lead. As winner of the 2007 Kraft Nabisco Championship, Pressel became the youngest women ever to win an LPGA major. The win also vaulted her into the top five of the Rolex World Rankings and qualified her for the ADT Championship,

the final event of the LPGA season, which earns $1 million for
the winner. "[It] seems like it's
been forever" since her first
LPGA appearance, Pressel told
the media after her win. "I've always had high hopes and dreams.
This is exciting."

Two months later, Pressel broke
the $1 million career earnings
mark at the McDonald's LPGA
Championship, finishing 14th.
Through her first 18 tournaments
of the 2007 season, she missed the
cut only twice and finished in the
top 10 seven times. This included a
tie for 10th at the U.S. Women's
Open and a second-place finish at
the Jamie Farr Owens Corning
Classic. In the latter tournament,
Pressel recorded her first hole-in-
one as a professional—the only
one shot during the competition's
four rounds. By the end of August
2007 she was eighth in the Rolex

*Pressel with the trophy
from her first major win—the
Dinah Shore Trophy from
the 2007 LPGA
Kraft Nabisco Championship.*

World Rankings and had earned a place on the 2007 Solheim Cup team, as
one of 12 golfers to represent the U.S. in competition against Europe.

Building a Pro Career

Pressel believes that with hard work and determination, she can have a long
career as a professional golfer. "I love to compete," she noted. "I love the
search for perfection. I'm constantly refining things, trying to be as perfect a
player as I can be." For instance, she admitted that that "putting is what I
need to practice the most," so she set up a track and practiced 100 putts in a
row. Strength and flexibility training are also important parts of her regimen.

Although Pressel is full of focus and control when it comes to her golf
game, she is not always so reserved when it comes to her emotions. She
cried tears of happiness during her victory at the Kraft Nabisco Championship and tears of frustration when she double-bogeyed her final hole at
the 2007 U.S. Women's to finish a 6-over-par round. Although tradition
dictates that golf players should be more restrained on the course, "I don't

think it's a bad thing at all, not only in my playing, but in relating to fans," Pressel said. "I don't think I'm going to change anytime soon." Her emotional style certainly hasn't hurt her appeal with fans, or her ability to win lucrative endorsements. In 2007 she had deals with Callaway Golf, Polo Ralph Lauren (their first American female athlete), Oakley sunglasses, and Gemisis cultured diamonds.

Pressel has also earned a reputation as a player who is not afraid to speak her mind. She gained a lot of publicity for her remarks about Michelle Wie, the sometimes controversial teen sensation who has played in men's PGA tournaments. Although Wie has millions of dollars in endorsements, she has yet to win a professional tournament. Pressel observed, "Michelle hasn't played a lot of junior golf, so she hasn't learned how to finish tournaments. She's obviously more interested in making cuts. But if you keep playing against players you can't beat, how are you going to learn to win?" When asked if she thought her comments were controversial, she responded that "people always have their own opinions and say what they want. Whether it's unfair or not, I don't know. That's just the way I am. I'm just being myself. I'm not going to hide anything because I have nothing to hide. I'm not going to sugarcoat it, that's for sure." (For more information on Wie, see *Biography Today*, Sep. 2004).

> "I know my mom wants me to keep chasing my dream and to be happy," Pressel said. "I'm where I want to be. And she's with me every day."

Pressel hasn't focused on Wie more than any other competitor. "We have an on-course rivalry, but are friendly both on and off the course," she explained in her blog. "Any comments I have made in the past about her were always about a general situation, never anything personal. But, if the media wants to build it up, it is probably a good thing for the LPGA Tour." Besides Pressel and Wie, there are several golfers in their teens and early 20s who are becoming prominent on the tour. "Everyone has their time, and our time is now," Pressel said. "We're bringing a lot of interest to the game. The ratings [for the Open] were way up. I just think it's fantastic for the game."

Professional golf is a game Pressel hopes to both dominate and champion in the future. "I want to be the best player in the world, definitely Hall of Fame, and see where it takes me," she has said. "I want to be influential, maybe help change the game a little bit, help change the face of the game:

nake it] a little more popular, maybe raise prize money." At a petite 5'5" ll, Pressel doesn't have the power to drive the ball as far as some of her ompetitors. She makes up for it with precision drives, a superb short ame, and careful putting—in short, she finds the greens and makes irdies. With the hard work and determination her family has inspired in er, she is likely to meet her goal. "I know my mom wants me to keep hasing my dream and to be happy," Pressel said. "I'm where I want to be. nd she's with me every day."

IOME AND FAMILY

Vhen not on tour, Pressel lives in her home town of Boca Raton, Florida, ith her grandparents, Herb and Evelyn Krickstein. She has lived with 1em since her mother's death in 2003; they accompany her when she is aveling on the LPGA Tour, while her father takes care of her two younger blings. While at home, she spends time with friends and her younger sib- ngs. She and her family also attend services at a local Jewish synagogue, here Pressel made her bat mitzvah.

IOBBIES AND OTHER INTERESTS

'ressel enjoys photography, computers, and using the newest electronic adgets (such as her Blackberry) to keep in touch with friends. She loves 1usic and enjoys alternative bands such as her favorite, Fall Out Boy, as ell as the occasional top-40 and hip hop artist. Pressel is innvolved with reast and ovarian cancer charities, including the Florida Hospital Cancer 1stitute's Kathryn Krickstein Pressel Memorial Fund, which is named after er late mother. In late 2005 she received the CoURagE Award from fellow olfer Cristie Kerr's charity Birdies for Breast Cancer. Pressel has also stated er intent to create her own charity golf event, perhaps as soon as 2008.

IONORS AND AWARDS

Jnior All-American First Team: 2003, 2004, 2005
3irls Rolex Junior Player of the Year (American Junior Golf Association): 2005
Jancy Lopez Award (American Junior Golf Association): 2006
Craft Nabisco Championship: 2007

'URTHER READING

'eriodicals

3altimore Sun, Feb. 16, 2006, p.E9
)etroit Free Press, July 6, 2005
3olf Digest, Feb. 2006, p.83

New York Times, June 6, 2007, p.D1
Palm Beach Post, Aug. 14, 2005
Philadelphia Inquirer, June 2, 2006
South Florida Sun-Sentinel, Nov. 8, 2004, p.A1; Aug. 8, 2005, p.C1; June 24, 2007
Sports Illustrated, May 28, 2001, p.G11; Aug. 8, 2005, p.52
Sports Illustrated for Kids, July 2007, p.42
USA Today, May 16, 2001, p.C3; Aug. 7, 2005; June 27, 2007, p.C3

Online Articles

http://sports.espn.go.com
   (ESPN, "Pressel Survives, Becomes Youngest to Win LPGA Major,"
   Apr. 1, 2007)
http://www.golfdigest.com
   (GolfWorld News & Tours, "Continuing Education," Feb. 3, 2006)
http://www.jewishtimes.com
   (Jewish Times, "They Punch, Putt, Dribble, Tackle and Skate and They're
   All Jewish," Mar. 16, 2007)

ADDRESS

Morgan Pressel
Ladies Professional Golf Association
100 International Golf Drive
Daytona Beach, FL. 32124-1092

WORLD WIDE WEB SITES

http://www.LPGA.com
http://www.callawaygolf.com

J. K. Rowling 1965-
British Children's Writer
Author of the Award-Winning *Harry Potter* Novels

[Editor's Note: J.K. Rowling was first profiled in Biography Today *in September 1999, after the publication of* Harry Potter and the Prisoner of Azkaban *and before the release of any of the movies. A lot has happened since then—in Rowling's life, and in Harry's— which is covered in this entry.]*

BIRTH

Joanne Kathleen (J. K.) Rowling (pronounced "rolling") was born on July 31, 1965, in Chipping Sodbury, a small town in

South Gloucestershire, England. Her parents, Peter and Anne Rowling, met on a train when they were both 18 years old and on their way to join the British Navy. Peter worked as an aircraft factory manager, and Anne was a lab technician. Rowling's birth name was simply Joanne; she added the name of her favorite grandmother, Kathleen, as her middle name later in life when her publisher wanted her to have another initial. Rowling has one younger sister, Dianne.

YOUTH

In describing her childhood, Rowling compares herself to one of the characters in her popular *Harry Potter* books. "By nature I am most like Hermione . . . or at least I was when I was younger." Rowling was considered "the smart one" while her sister was "the pretty one." As children, they were best friends even though they fought a lot.

> ———— **"** ————
>
> *In describing her childhood, Rowling compares herself to one of the characters in her popular* **Harry Potter** *books.* *"By nature I am most like Hermione . . . or at least I was when I was younger."*
>
> ———— **"** ————

When Rowling was four years old her family moved to the town of Winterbourne just outside Bristol, England. There she had lots of friends in the neighborhood, including a brother and sister whose surname was Potter, a name that Rowling liked. As a young child, she began making up elaborate stories and plays starring herself, her sister, and their friends. She first began writing stories around age six. Most of the stories she wrote at that time featured rabbits, because she wanted a rabbit as a pet.

When Rowling was nine years old, her family moved again. Her parents wanted to live farther out in the countryside, so they settled in the village of Tutshill, near Chepstow in Wales. Wales is one of the four countries that make up the United Kingdom, along with England, Scotland, and Northern Ireland. Wales is known for its 400 castles, its ancient legends, and its tongue-twisting place names. Rowling would later draw on her experiences growing up in Wales when creating the magical world of Harry Potter.

EDUCATION

Rowling enjoyed going to school and generally did well as a student, except for a period in elementary school. The elementary school where she started out, in Winterbourne, did not prepare her for her new school in Tutshill. On Rowling's first day in her new school, her teacher gave her a math test to determine where to place her in the class. Rowling got every question wrong because she did not know anything about fractions. The teacher placed her at a desk as far away from her own as possible. Rowling spent that year primarily focused on carving a hole in the wooden desktop with the point of her geometry compass.

Things improved greatly when Rowling was 11 years old and was able to attend Wyedean Comprehensive School in Chepstow. There she struck up a friendship with Sean Harris, who was the first person with whom she shared her dream of becoming a writer and also the person who most believed that she could achieve that goal. When Harris learned to drive, he often took Rowling for rides in his Ford Anglia. "That turquoise and white car meant freedom. . . . Some of the happiest memories of my teenage years involve zooming off into the darkness in Sean's car." Her second book, *Harry Potter and the Chamber of Secrets,* is dedicated to him.

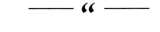

"I think most people believe, deep down, that their mothers are indestructible; it was a terrible shock to hear that she had an incurable illness, but even then, I did not fully realize what the diagnosis might mean."

By this time in her life, Rowling loved writing more than anything else. During lunchtime at school, she entertained her friends by telling stories starring themselves as the courageous heroes of dangerous—and sometimes silly—adventures. But Rowling still didn't show anyone most of the things she had written. She remembers being too shy to let anyone see her work.

In 1980, when Rowling was 15 years old, her mother, Anne Rowling, became very ill and was diagnosed with multiple sclerosis. Multiple sclerosis (MS) is an incurable disease of the central nervous system that affects the brain and spinal cord. It can eventually result in numbness and loss of muscle control, balance, and vision. Some people with MS have periods of time during which the disease stops getting worse, but Anne Rowling gradually became weaker and more seriously ill. Her illness had a huge impact on Rowling. "I think most people believe, deep down, that their mothers are indestructible; it was a terrible shock to hear that she had an incurable illness, but even then, I did not fully realize what the diagnosis might mean."

Rowling finished secondary school in 1983 and went on to study at the University of Exeter in southern England. She wanted to study English literature, but took her parents' advice and studied French instead. Although she later said that choice was a mistake, it did provide her with the opportunity to live in Paris for one year. She received a Bachelor of Arts (BA) degree in French from the University of Exeter in 1987.

——— **“** ———

On a crowded train, the character of Harry Potter "simply fell into my head," Rowling said. "I didn't have a functioning pen with me, and I was too shy to ask anybody if I could borrow one. . . . I simply sat and thought, for four hours, and all the details bubbled up in my brain, and this scrawny, black-haired, bespectacled boy who didn't know he was a wizard became more and more real to me."

——— **”** ———

CAREER HIGHLIGHTS

After college, Rowling continued to write stories and also began writing two novels while working a series of different jobs in London, England. The longest job she held was as a secretary with the international human rights organization Amnesty International. Rowling has described herself as "the worst secretary ever." She recalled not paying very much attention in business meetings because she was too busy making notes of her story ideas. "This is a problem when you are supposed to be taking the minutes of the meeting. . . . I'm not proud of that. I don't think it's charming and eccentric. I really should have been better at it, but I really am just all over the place when it comes to organizing myself."

Creating Harry Potter

In 1990, Rowling decided to move to the city of Manchester, England. On a crowded train back to London after a weekend spent looking for a place to live, the character of Harry Potter "simply fell into my head." In her web site biography, she wrote, "I didn't have a functioning pen with me, and I was too shy to ask anybody if I could borrow one. . . . I simply sat and thought, for four hours, and all the details bubbled up in my brain, and this scrawny, black-haired, bespectacled boy who didn't know he was a wizard became more and more real to me." When she got home that evening, Rowling began to write *Harry Potter and the*

Rowling with Daniel Radcliffe, who would bring her creation to life.

Philosopher's Stone (published in the United States as *Harry Potter and the Sorcerer's Stone*).

Rowling's story of Harry Potter focuses on a young orphan who learns on his 11th birthday that he has a magical legacy and must attend a special school for wizards. From the very beginning, Rowling imagined a series of seven books that would follow the life and adventures of Harry from age 11 to age 18. During those years, he would discover many things about himself. In between the challenges of schoolwork and sports, Harry and his friends Ron and Hermione would fight monsters and evil wizards, prevent magical disasters, and survive many narrow escapes while saving the wizarding world from the fearsome Voldemort.

By the end of 1990, Rowling had made significant progress on the first Harry Potter book. She had a good start on the story and lots of ideas for the books that would follow. Then on December 30, 1990, her mother died.

Rowling was devastated. Her mother was only 45 years old, and Rowling never thought she would die so young. "It was a terrible time. . . . I remember feeling as though there was a paving slab pressing down upon my chest, a literal pain in my heart."

In 1991 Rowling was still struggling with grief over her mother's death. Wanting to get away, she took a job teaching English in Portugal and continued working on her book. The storyline had changed since her mother's death and now included much more detail about Harry's feelings for his own parents. In Portugal, Rowling wrote her favorite chapter of the book, "The Mirror of Erised," in which Harry discovers images of his long-dead parents.

> —— " ——
>
> *"From that very first idea, I [envisioned] a series of seven books—each one charting a year of Harry's life whilst he is a student at Hogwarts School of Witchcraft and Wizardry," Rowling explained. "And I wanted to fully sketch the plots of all the stories and get the essential characteristics of my principal characters before I actually started writing the books in detail."*
>
> —— " ——

Also during this time, Rowling was briefly married to a Portuguese man and gave birth to her daughter Jessica. When the marriage ended in divorce in 1994, Rowling moved with her daughter to Edinburgh, Scotland, to live near her sister. She had accepted a teaching position and wanted to finish writing the book before her new job began. She was afraid that once she started working full-time again, she wouldn't have enough time for writing. "And so I set to work in a kind of frenzy, determined to finish the book and at least try and get it published. Whenever Jessica fell asleep in her pushchair [stroller] I would dash to the nearest café and write like mad. I wrote nearly every evening. Then I had to type the whole thing out myself. Sometimes I actually hated the book, even while I loved it."

From her first thought of Harry while riding the train to London to the last bit of writing in Edinburgh, it ultimately took Rowling five years to finish the book. "The reason so much time slipped by was because, from that very first idea, I [envisioned] a series of seven books—each one charting a year of Harry's life whilst he is a student at Hogwarts School of Witchcraft and Wizardry," she explained. "And I wanted to fully sketch the plots of all the stories and get the essential characteristics of my principal characters before I actually started writing the books in detail." Because Rowling always knew how the story of Harry Potter would end, she never thought of them as children's books.

Once Rowling found a literary agent to help her, it took over a year of rejections before she was offered a publishing contract. In August 1996, she signed an agreement with a British publisher. "The moment I found out that Harry would be published was one of the best of my life." Her excitement could not be diminished, not even by the career advice she got from her first editor. The editor warned Rowling that she wouldn't make any money by writing children's books, so she should get a regular job and not try to depend on Harry Potter to earn her living.

But just a few months after her book was accepted for publication in England, a U.S. publisher also bought the publishing rights. Rowling was offered $100,000 for the rights to publish the first Harry Potter book in the United States. This was the highest fee ever paid for a first novel by a children's book author, and it allowed Rowling to quit her teaching job to concentrate on writing Harry's story full time. And so Harry Potter began breaking publishing records before the first copies of the first book were even printed.

Book 1: *Harry Potter and the Sorcerer's Stone*

Harry Potter and the Philosopher's Stone was released in England in 1997 and followed by the U.S. version, *Harry Potter and the Sorcerer's Stone,* in 1998. In this first Harry Potter book, readers are introduced to an unlikely hero. Harry is an orphan boy who lives in a closet under the stairs in the home of his mean-spirited aunt and uncle who only reluctantly took him in. He leads a completely miserable life in which he is constantly bullied by his cousin Dudley and treated as a servant by his aunt and uncle. The only remarkable thing about Harry is the mysterious lightning bolt scar on his forehead.

Then, on his 11th birthday, Harry receives a letter that sets off a chain of events leading to the revelation that he is, in fact, a wizard. His parents were not killed in a car accident as he had been told. They were murdered by an evil wizard named Voldemort. Harry himself is a legend among wizards because he is the only person ever to have survived a direct attack by Voldemort. With this new information, Harry's life is changed forever. He is whisked away on a flying motorcycle to Hogwarts School of Witchcraft and Wizardry, where he studies charms, potions, and the history of magic. He forms friendships with Ron and Hermione, and together they investigate the many forbidden secrets of Hogwarts, play Quidditch, battle evil

The first book in the saga of Harry Potter.

forces, and uncover the secret of the sorcerer's stone. In another series of revelations, Harry discovers the true meaning of his scar.

Rowling's first book became a runaway bestseller. Harry Potter was met with rave reviews by book critics in England as well as in the U.S. A reviewer for the *Times* of London praised Rowling as "a sparkling new author brimming with delicious ideas, glorious characters, and witty dialogue," while the *Sunday Times* called the novel a "very funny, imaginative, magical story, for anyone from ten to adulthood." American book reviewers called Rowling's writing "charming, readable, delightful" and "brilliantly imagined and written." *Harry Potter and the Sorcerer's Stone* was a spectacular beginning to what would become a huge international publishing sensation.

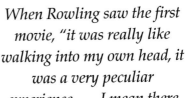

When Rowling saw the first movie, "it was really like walking into my own head, it was a very peculiar experience. . . . I mean there are obviously things that are not the same as the books but that is because if you did every scene in the book and translated that into films, the films would be about 24 hours each."

The movie version of *Harry Potter and the Sorcerer's Stone* was released in 2001, bringing the world of Harry Potter to life on the screen. Although initially reluctant to allow her books to be made into movies, Rowling is happy with the films. "It was really like walking into my own head, it was a very peculiar experience. . . . I mean there are obviously things that are not the same as the books but that is because if you did every scene in the book and translated that into films, the films would be about 24 hours each. . . . By and large they meet my expectations."

Book 2: *Harry Potter and the Chamber of Secrets*

Harry Potter and the Chamber of Secrets was published in 1998, and the movie version of the book was released in 2002. Detailing Harry's exploits during his second year at Hogwarts, the storyline centers on a terrible monster that has escaped from the Chamber of Secrets and is turning Hogwarts students to stone. While dealing with flying cars, angry willow trees, various bullies and ghosts, and the suspicions of many Hogwarts students that he is to blame for the escaped monster, Harry must confront the evil Voldemort and solve the mystery. Harry's adventures and mishaps along the way prompt Hogwarts Headmaster Dumbledore to offer the advice that gives a hint of our hero's future: "It is our choices, Harry, that show what we truly are, far more than our abilities."

Proving just as popular as the first book, *Harry Potter and the Chamber of Secrets* became the best-selling book in the U.S. as soon as it was released. *Publisher's Weekly* called the book "even more inventive than *Harry Potter and the Sorcerer's Stone.*" Readers and critics alike praised Rowling's story as imaginative, funny, suspenseful, and truly magical.

Book 3: *Harry Potter and the Prisoner of Azkaban*

Harry Potter and the Prisoner of Azkaban, released in 1999 with the movie version following in 2004, is the third installment in the series. In this story, Harry learns about the wizard prison called Azkaban, which is guarded by the frightening and ghoulish Dementors. Harry's godfather Sirius Black, who is believed to have helped Voldemort murder Harry's parents, escapes from prison and is looking for Harry. Harry and his friends study Defense Against the Dark Arts and learn how to perform the difficult Patronus charm. As the story unfolds, Harry learns more about his parents while encountering werewolves, mysterious disappearances, daring rescues, and surprising friendships. Harry must also once again confront the power of evil.

By the time the third Harry Potter book was published, the series had attracted readers of all ages, all of whom expressed delight with the newest story. The book was greeted by critics as an enthralling, thrilling addition to the series. And Harry Potter fans were already looking forward to more from Rowling, who said in 1999, "I've actually got the final chapter of book seven written, just for my own satisfaction so I know where I'm going."

Book 4: *Harry Potter and the Goblet of Fire*

Harry Potter and the Goblet of Fire, released in 2000 with the movie version following in 2005, chronicles Harry's fourth year at Hogwarts. The school is hosting the Triwizard Tournament, and although he is technically too young to participate, Harry is drawn into the competition. The tournament events place competitors in grave danger, and advanced magical skills are required to escape injury. Readers are also introduced to the Quidditch World Cup, magical transportation by portkey, and the terrible Death Eaters. The story rushes toward a shocking conclusion in which Harry again confronts Voldemort in battle, and an important character is killed. Rowling has admitted to crying while writing the death scene, but she persevered because she felt the death was critical to the storyline.

Top: Harry with the Dursleys, as he learns he is going to Hogwarts.

Center: Hermione, Harry, and Ron, with Scabbers.

Bottom: Harry and the sorting hat.

Rowling struggled with the process of writing *Harry Potter and the Goblet of Fire*, particularly Chapter 9, "The Dark Mark," which introduces the Death Eaters. "The worst ever was 13 different versions. . . . I hated that chapter so much; at one point, I thought of missing it out altogether and just putting in a page saying 'Chapter 9 was too difficult' and going straight to Chapter 10." Her hard work paid off, and the book received glowing reviews. A *Newsweek* book reviewer called the book astonishing and "the best Potter book yet." The book was also praised as complex, finely plotted, and suspenseful but funny.

> ————— **"** —————
>
> *Rowling said in 1999, "I've actually got the final chapter of book seven written, just for my own satisfaction so I know where I'm going."*
>
> ————— **"** —————

The phenomenon of midnight bookstore release parties began with the publication of *Harry Potter and the Goblet of Fire*. Eager fans waited in line for hours to get their copies of the latest Harry Potter book at the stroke of midnight. The book sold an unprecedented three million copies in the first 48 hours of release. *Harry Potter and the Goblet of Fire* became the fastest-selling book in history, a distinction that was later eclipsed by sales of subsequent Harry Potter titles.

Quidditch Through the Ages and *Fantastic Beasts and Where to Find Them*

In 2001, Rowling published a special supplement to the Harry Potter series as a fundraiser for the charitable organization Comic Relief U.K. *Quidditch Through the Ages* was written by Rowling under the pen name Kennilworthy Whisp, while *Fantastic Beasts and Where to Find Them*, also written by Rowling, was published under the pen name Newt Scamander. The two books were designed to look like Hogwarts textbooks. The titles were a huge hit with fans who by now wanted to know every detail of Harry's life and the magical world of wizards.

Book 5: *Harry Potter and the Order of the Phoenix*

Harry Potter and the Order of the Phoenix details Harry's fifth year at Hogwarts and was released in 2003, with the movie version following in 2006. As Harry grows into adolescence, he becomes more serious and angry. Dementors attack Harry and his cousin Dudley, and Harry is suspended from Hogwarts and must undergo a disciplinary hearing at the Ministry of Magic. He begins having horrible nightmares that he doesn't understand.

Top: *A pensive Dumbledore.*

Middle: *Snape in his classroom, with wand at the ready.*

Bottom: *Harry, Hermione, and Ron, with the golden egg.*

Harry learns about the Order of the Phoenix, a group working against Voldemort, and gets more information about his parents, who were early members of the Order. New characters are introduced, and Hogwarts comes under the control of the spiteful Professor Umbridge. A battle with the Death Eaters ensues, and another important character is killed. Harry learns of a prophecy made before he was born, and the stage is set for the final two books of the series.

Anticipation of *Harry Potter and the Order of the Phoenix* had reached fever pitch by the time the book was released. One reviewer writing for *January* magazine noted that "this novel is no longer children's literature" and continued that the book was "written on several levels for a wide variety of readers." Rowling's work in creating the Harry Potter series was also praised as a richly realized universe that became more complex with each book.

Book 6: *Harry Potter and the Half-Blood Prince*

Harry Potter and the Half-Blood Prince was released in 2005 and immediately called "the darkest and most unsettling installment yet" by the *New York Times.* In this story, Harry learns of the existence of the half-blood prince through a mysterious book that helps him pass his Hogwarts exams. Voldemort and the Death Eaters commit a string of heinous murders and the full-blown wizard war causes several disasters in the Muggle world. Dumbledore tells Harry about the horcruxes, which if destroyed will also kill Voldemort. The book's tragic and shocking ending leads Harry to finally understand his life's destiny.

With the publication of the sixth book, critics continued to rave about the Harry Potter series. A *National Review* critic called the book a "breathless story of heroism, intrigue, and cowardly villainy" and praised the intricate storyline, engaging mystery, and suspense. A reviewer for *Booklist* praised Rowling as a writer who "blends literature, mythology, folklore, and religion into a delectable stew." The publication of *Harry Potter and the Half-Blood Prince* set a new world record for the number of copies ordered for the first printing of a book. But that record would ultimately be broken by the final book in the series.

Book 7: *Harry Potter and the Deathly Hallows*

The final installment of the Harry Potter series, *Harry Potter and the Deathly Hallows,* was the most highly anticipated book in history by the time it was released in 2007. The story opens with a raging war in the wizarding world. Voldemort is gaining control of the Ministry of Magic and hunting Muggles and half-blood wizards. Harry is named "Undesirable Number One" and goes into hiding along with Ron and Hermione. Together they search for the mysterious horcruxes in an attempt to defeat Voldemort once and for all. They also try to find the Hallows, a legendary collection of items that will make whoever possesses them the master of death. Mayhem, betrayal, mistrust, reversals of alliance, and bitter clashes unfold. Beloved characters die, but Harry learns that love can triumph over death—although the cost is sometimes high.

The public frenzy surrounding the publication of the final Harry Potter book required an elaborate secrecy campaign to prevent spoilers—advance information about how the story would end. *Harry Potter and the Deathly Hallows* had the largest first printing of any book in history, and the more copies of a book that are printed, the greater the risk of spoilers. Everyone who came into contact with the book before its release date of July 21, 2007, was legally bound to secrecy. Only a limited number of people were granted access to the manuscript during the editing process. When Rowling finished her final revisions to the book, the editor assigned to deliver the manuscript to the publisher sat on it during the long flight from London to New York. As copies of the books were printed, they were automatically wrapped in black plastic and loaded onto locked trucks with electronic devices that tracked their location at all times. Libraries and bookstore managers who received the advance shipments of books were required to sign a security agreement as well as provide their names and contact information. Many bookstores and libraries that received their copies days in advance hid the books to prevent them from being stolen.

——— " ———

"If I can credit myself with anything, it has been to make it cool for young people to start reading again. And in this day and age when books have to fight it out with such diversions as Gameboy and Pokemon, that alone gives me more pleasure than anything."

——— " ———

When readers and critics finally had access to the book, they were not disappointed. The *Washington Post* called the series finale "exhilarating but also exhausting . . . spectacularly complex." A *Chicago Tribune* reviewer described the story as "dark, rich, sophisticated, packed with action." Fans all over the world celebrated the seventh and final book—and immediately began guessing what Rowling would write next. Rowling addressed that

The publication of the last book was a moment of great joy and sadness for Rowling's fans, who were excited to read the story but sorry to have it end.

question by saying, "I definitely have thought about it, but I've made no decisions at all. I will definitely be writing. I literally don't quite feel right if I haven't written for awhile. A week is about as long as I can go without getting extremely edgy. . . . It really is a compulsion. Yeah, so I have ideas, but they could all be rubbish."

Rowling's Harry Potter books have been translated into more than 60 languages and distributed in 200 countries around the world. More than a quarter of a billion copies have been sold, and the characters have been licensed for use in hundred of toys and video games. Although the final book has already been published, Harry Potter's popularity shows no signs of waning as fans anticipate the release of the movie versions of the last two books.

"I don't think there's any subject matter that can't be explored in literature. Any subject matter at all. I really hate censorship. People have the right to decide what they want their children to read, but in my opinion they do not have the right to tell other people's children what they should read."

Time magazine called Harry Potter the most popular children's series ever written and said that Rowling "gets everything right, writes as though she knows what it is to be 13 years old and anxious or shocked at discovering what you can actually do if you try." One *Time* book reviewer observed, "Parents report reading levels jumping by four grades in two years. They cannot quite believe this gift, that for an entire generation of children, the most powerful entertainment experience of their lives comes not on a screen or a monitor or a disc but on a page." Rowling responded by saying, "If I can credit myself with anything, it has been to make it cool for young people to start reading again. And in this day and age when books have to fight it out with such diversions as Gameboy and Pokemon, that alone gives me more pleasure than anything."

Responding to Controversy

In spite of the worldwide Harry Potter phenomenon, not everyone is happy with Rowling's creation. The American Library Association reports that the Harry Potter books are the most challenged books in the United States, meaning that many people have requested that the books be banned from libraries and schools. Some religious organizations believe the books promote witchcraft and Satanism. One mother told a reporter that the Potter books have "an anti-Christian agenda." "My prayer is that parents would wake up, that the subtle way this is presented as harmless fantasy would be exposed for what it really is—a subtle indoctrination into anti-Christian values," she said. "The kids are being introduced to a cult and witchcraft practices."

> "The Potter books in general are a prolonged argument for tolerance, a prolonged plea for an end to bigotry, and I think it's one of the reasons that some people don't like the books, but I think that it's a very healthy message to pass on to younger people."

Rowling responds to the accusations by saying, "These extreme religious folk have just missed the point so spectacularly. I think the Harry books are actually very moral, but some people just object to witchcraft being mentioned in a children's book. Unfortunately, if such extremist views were to prevail, we would have to lose a lot of classic children's fiction. . . . I don't think there's any subject matter that can't be explored in literature. Any subject matter at all. I really hate censorship. People have the right to decide what they want their children to read, but in my opinion they do not have the right to tell other people's children what they should read."

An additional subject of controversy came up in late 2007, when Rowling appeared at Carnegie Hall in New York City. She read from *Harry Potter and the Deathly Hallows* and answered questions from the audience. She revealed several interesting tidbits about the characters—that Neville Longbottom married Hufflepuff Hannah Abbott, who became the landlady at the Leaky Cauldron pub; that Hagrid never married, since it was so difficult for him to meet women his size; and that Professor Dumbledore was gay and that the great love of his life had been his friend Grindelwald. The revelation about Dumbledore excited and intrigued many of her fans, but angered and inflamed those who object to her works. For Rowling, however, it was never an issue. "The Potter books in general are a prolonged argument for tolerance, a prolonged plea for an end to bigotry, and I think it's one of the reasons that some people don't like the books, but I think that it's a very healthy message to pass on to younger people." As Dumbledore himself said, "Differences of habit and language are nothing at all if our aims are identical and our hearts are open."

Rowling signing a copy of Harry Potter and the Deathly Hallows *for a student in New Orleans.*

Living with Fame

Thanks to Harry Potter, Rowling has become one of the wealthiest women in the world. She is the first person ever to become a billionaire by writing books. She has given countless interviews and appeared on television and radio programs around the world. For an entire decade Rowling was Amazon.com's No. 1 Top Selling Author. In spite of her fame, however, Rowling is almost unrecognizable in public.

"It's really the exception rather than the norm that anyone would approach me. . . . There was a phase when I had journalists at my front door quite a lot, and that was quite horrible. That was not something that I ever anticipated happening to me, and it's not pleasant, whoever you are. But I don't want to whine, because this was my life's ambition, and I've overshot the mark so hugely. . . . I am an extraordinarily lucky person, doing what I love best in the world."

At one time Rowling was too shy to show her writing to even one person, but that has now become her favorite part of being a published author. "I have found readings to be the most fantastic experience. I think part of that satisfaction comes from the fact that I was writing the books in secret for so long that I never talked to anyone about them. For five years I was the only person who had read a word of Harry Potter, and the only person who knew all these things about Harry's world and his friends. So the novelty of sitting in front of all these hundreds of people in bookshops all over the world and hearing them laugh, answering their questions and discussing my characters still hasn't worn off."

MARRIAGE AND FAMILY

Rowling married Jorge Aranes on October 16, 1992. They had one daughter, Jessica. The marriage ended in divorce on November 30, 1993. On December 26, 2001, Rowling married Neil Murray. They have a son, David, and a daughter, Mackenzie. Rowling lives with her husband and three children near the small town of Aberfeldy, Scotland.

WRITINGS

Harry Potter and the Philosopher's Stone, 1997 (British title)
Harry Potter and the Sorcerer's Stone, 1998 (U.S. title)
Harry Potter and the Chamber of Secrets, 1998
Harry Potter and the Prisoner of Azkaban, 1999
Harry Potter and the Goblet of Fire, 2000
Quidditch Through the Ages, 2001 (under name Kennilworthy Whisp)
Fantastic Beasts and Where to Find Them, 2001 (under name Newt Scamander)
Harry Potter and the Order of the Phoenix, 2003
Harry Potter and the Half-Blood Prince, 2005
Harry Potter and the Deathly Hallows, 2007

HONORS AND AWARDS

Children's Book of the Year (British Book Awards): 1997, for *Harry Potter and the Philosopher's Stone*

Gold Winner, Nestle Book Prize (Nestle): 1997, for *Harry Potter and the Philosopher's Stone;* 1998, for *Harry Potter and the Chamber of Secrets;* 1999, for *Harry Potter and the Prisoner of Azkaban*

Carnegie Medal: 1997, for *Harry Potter and the Philosopher's Stone*

Anne Spencer Lindbergh Prize in Children's Literature: 1997-98, for *Harry Potter and the Sorcerer's Stone*

Best Book designation (*Publisher's Weekly*): 1998, for *Harry Potter and the Sorcerer's Stone*

Editor's Choice designation (*Booklist*): 1998, for *Harry Potter and the Sorcerer's Stone;* 1999, for *Harry Potter and the Chamber of Secrets;* 1999, for *Harry Potter and the Prisoner of Azkaban*

Notable Book designation (American Library Association): 1998, for *Harry Potter and the Sorcerer's Stone*

Best Book of the Year (New York Public Library): 1998, for *Harry Potter and the Sorcerer's Stone*

Best Book for Young Adults (American Library Association): 1999, for *Harry Potter and the Chamber of Secrets*

Best Book of the Year (*School Library Journal*): 1999, for *Harry Potter and the Chamber of Secrets*

Whitbread Prize for Children's Literature: 1999, for *Harry Potter and the Prisoner of Azkaban*

W.H. Smith Children's Book of the Year Award: 2000, for *Harry Potter and the Goblet of Fire*

Hugo Award (World Science Fiction Society): 2001, Best Novel, for *Harry Potter and the Goblet of Fire*

Officer of the Most Excellent Order of the British Empire (O.B.E.) (Charles, Prince of Wales): 2001, for services to children's literature

Scottish Arts Council Book Award: 2001, for *Harry Potter and the Goblet of Fire*

Rebecca Caudill Young Reader's Award: 2001, for *Harry Potter and the Sorcerer's Stone*

Bram Stoker Award: 2003, Young Readers Category, for *Harry Potter and the Order of the Phoenix*

W.H. Smith Book Award: 2004, fiction category, for *Harry Potter and the Order of the Phoenix*

Book of the Year (Quill Book Awards): 2006, for *Harry Potter and the Half-Blood Prince*

Book of the Year (British Book Awards): 2006, for *Harry Potter and the Half-Blood Prince*

Best Book Award (Kids' Choice Awards): 2006, for the *Harry Potter* series

Rave Award (*Wired*): 2007

FURTHER READING

Books

Authors and Artists for Young Adults, Vol. 34, 2000
Major Authors and Illustrators for Children and Young Adults, 2002
Who's Who in America, 2007

Periodicals

Chicago Tribune, July 22, 2007, p.C1
Entertainment Weekly, Nov. 22, 2002, p.49; June 11, 2004, p.93; Nov. 11,
  2005, p.22; July 20, 2007, p.30; Nov. 2, 2007, p.72; Nov. 30, 2007, p. 34
New York Times, July 10, 2007, p.E1
Newsweek, July 10, 2000, p.56; June 30, 2003, p.50
Time, Apr. 12, 1999, p.86; Sep. 20, 1999, p.66; July 17, 2000, p.70; Oct. 30,
  2000, p.108; Dec. 25, 2000, p.116; June 23, 2003, p.60; June 30, 2003, p.60;
  June 7, 2004, p.117; July 25, 2005, p.60; July 9, 2007
Toronto Star, Nov. 3, 2001, p.A31
USA Today, July 7, 2005; July 10, 2007, p.D2
Washington Post, July 22, 2007, p.D1

Online Articles

http://www.januarymagazine.com/kidsbooks/potter5.html
  (January magazine, "Growing Up With Harry," July 2003)
http://www.msnbc.msn.com/id/20026225
  (MSNBC.com, "Rowling: I Wanted to Kill Parents," July 29, 2007)
http://today.msnbc.msn.com/id/19991430
  (MSNBC.com, "Rowling Regret: Never Told Mom About *Potter,*" July 27,
  2007)

ADDRESS

J.K. Rowling
Scholastic
555 Broadway
New York, NY 10012

WORLD WIDE WEB SITES

http://www.jkrowling.com
http://www.scholastic.com/harrypotter/books/author
http://www.bloomsbury.com/authors

Karen P. Tandy 1953-

American Former Administrator of the Federal
Drug Enforcement Agency (DEA)
First Woman to Lead the U.S. Battle against
Illegal Drugs

BIRTH

Karen Patrice Tandy was born on October 24, 1953, in Fort
Worth, Texas, to William C. Tandy Jr., a communications technician for Southern Bell Telephone Co., and Juanita Jo Tandy, a
secretary. She has a sister, Pamela.

YOUTH AND EDUCATION

Tandy grew up in Hurst, Texas. Years later, she said that her parents worked hard so "my sister and I achieved the higher education that eluded them." She described her father as "a blue collar worker" and her mother as "a hero and a role model of her own, for she was a working mother at a time when society frowned on working mothers."

Tandy attended Lawrence Dale Bell High School (better known as L.D. Bell) in Hurst, where she was a member of the National Honor Society and voted Miss L.D. Bell. After graduating from high school in 1971, she attended Texas Tech University in Lubbock, Texas. Tandy earned a Bachelor of Science (BS) degree in education in 1971. She continued her education at Texas Tech's School of Law, where she became president of the student bar association. Her election to that prestigious college position "reflected the respect and confidence that the rest of us had in Karen, and her willingness to step up and be a leader," said a former classmate, Walter Dean, who is dean of the Texas Tech Law School. Tandy received her law degree in 1977.

> *Tandy described her mother as "a hero and a role model of her own, for she was a working mother at a time when society frowned on working mothers."*

FIRST JOBS

Tandy began her legal career by serving as a judicial clerk for a federal judge in Texas. Judicial clerks typically assist judges by researching the legal backgrounds of pending cases. During her time as a clerk, Tandy came into contact with the assistant district attorneys who were prosecuting criminals, and she became interested in their work. "I decided that is what I wanted to do with my life," she said. "I had thought I would stay in Texas, but one of the potential employers I interviewed with told me that women didn't have the killer instinct to be criminal prosecutors. That caused me to look to the Department of Justice and move to Washington."

CAREER HIGHLIGHTS

In 1979, Tandy began working for the Department of Justice. The DOJ is the nation's highest law-enforcement agency, responsible for enforcing federal laws. Many separate agencies make up the DOJ, including the

Drug Enforcement Administration (DEA), the Federal Bureau of Investigation (FBI), the U.S. Marshals, and others. Agencies in the DOJ both investigate crimes and prosecute criminals in court.

At the Department of Justice, Tandy's first assignment was as an assistant United States attorney in the Eastern District of Virginia and in the Western District of Washington, DC. She worked on the prosecution of cases involving illegal drugs and violent crimes. She soon began her steady movement up the ranks, earning many promotions. Over the next 11 years, Tandy held several leadership positions, including Chief of the Narcotics Division and Lead Attorney for the Organized and Crime Drug Division Enforcement Task Forces.

> "
>
> *Tandy first became interested in becoming a prosecutor while working as a law clerk. "I had thought I would stay in Texas, but one of the potential employers I interviewed with told me that women didn't have the killer instinct to be criminal prosecutors. That caused me to look to the Department of Justice and move to Washington."*
>
> "

When she moved to the Justice Department's Criminal Division in 1990, Tandy broadened her work in drug-related prosecutions. She became an expert in forfeiture law, which is the government's right to seize property gained by, or connected to, illegal activity. She was named Deputy Chief of the Narcotics and Dangerous Drug Section, and her duties included supervising narcotic prosecutions and drug wiretap investigations nationwide. During this time, Tandy developed a reputation for taking a hard-line approach against drug users and sellers. In 2001, she was named Associate Deputy Attorney General, a position that gave her responsibility for developing anti-drug enforcement policies across the country.

Nomination by President Bush

Tandy's biggest promotion came in 2003, when President George W. Bush nominated her to be the Administrator of the Drug Enforcement Agency (DEA). The DEA was created in 1973 to coordinate enforcement of federal drug laws. The Agency is a division of the Justice Department and has an annual budget of $2.2 billion, employs approximately 11,000 people, and has 237 offices throughout the U.S. as well as 80 offices in 58 foreign countries.

Tandy with her husband, Steve Pomerantz, during her swearing-in ceremony as the new adminstrator for the DEA.

Becoming the head of a federal agency requires confirmation by the U.S. Senate. Tandy was questioned first by the members of the U.S. Senate Judiciary Committee, who had to approve her nomination before the full Senate could vote on it. Tandy said that a major focus of her leadership at the DEA would be to fight international drug traffickers, many of whom smuggle drugs into the United States. "A key piece in this is developing our partnerships overseas, so we can work together hand and glove," she said.

Tandy's appearance before the committee prompted a discussion about the controversial issue of medical marijuana. Many patients who suffer from such chronic or life-threatening illnesses as cancer, multiple sclerosis, and glaucoma say that smoking marijuana helps ease their severe pain. These patients are able to obtain marijuana by getting a medical prescription from their doctor. As a result, nine states—Alaska, California, Colorado, Hawaii, Maine, Maryland, Nevada, Oregon, and Washington—either do not arrest patients or providers of medical marijuana, or just impose a small fine for violations.

But since the law banning the use of marijuana is a federal statute, the DEA has continued to make arrests for medical-marijuana possession or its sale, even in the nine states with lenient laws. Two Democratic senators on the Judiciary Committee—Dianne Feinstein of California and Dick Durbin of Illinois—wanted to know if Tandy supported this policy. Tandy stated emphatically that she did. In a written statement to the committee, she said, "If I am confirmed as administrator of the DEA, it will be my duty to see the uniform enforcement of federal law. I do not believe that it would be consistent with that duty for me to support a moratorium on enforcement of this law, or any law, in selected areas of the country."

In her Senate testimony, Tandy disputed the position that marijuana is medically beneficial. The active ingredient in marijuana, tetrahydrocannabinol (THC), has been proven effective when processed into a federally approved pill called Marinol, she stated. But "marijuana itself, however, has not been shown to have medical benefits," Tandy argued. Senators Feinstein and Durbin disagreed and submitted several published studies showing the medical benefits of marijuana into the Judiciary Committee's official record.

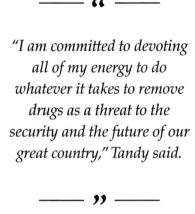

"I am committed to devoting all of my energy to do whatever it takes to remove drugs as a threat to the security and the future of our great country," Tandy said.

Tandy's nomination was ultimately approved by the committee, and its chairman, Sen. Orrin G. Hatch, R-Utah, praised her "long and impressive 25-year career with the Department of Justice."

Becoming DEA Administrator

On August 2, 2003, Tandy was confirmed as DEA Administrator without dissent by the entire Senate. She promised "proactive and bold leadership" in the fight to eliminate drug-smuggling operations. "I am committed to devoting all of my energy to do whatever it takes to remove drugs as a threat to the security and the future of our great country," she said.

As DEA Administrator, Tandy was charged with enforcing the laws related to drugs and other controlled substances. She was also responsible for bringing to the criminal justice system any individuals or organizations involved in growing, manufacturing, or distributing drugs. In addition, she was charged with investigating and prosecuting any violators of controlled substance laws, including criminals and drug gangs; running a national drug intelligence program, in conjunction with other agencies; seizing assets from drug trafficking; coordinating with other U.S. law enforcement agencies, as well as foreign governments, to enforce drug laws and reduce drug availability; and working with such international organizations as Interpol and the United Nations on drug-control programs.

The War against Methamphetamine

The increase in the use of methamphetamine (commonly called meth) is one of the most significant challenges facing the DEA and other law enforcement agencies around the U.S. Meth can be smoked, snorted, injected, or taken orally. It comes in the form of crystal-like powder or rock-like chunks. It can be made in a fairly simple lab, and labs have even been set up in people's homes. Before it is sold, the drug is mixed with a number of ingredients, most often the decongestant agents pseudophedrine or ephedrine—but in some cases with household-cleaning ingredients or even battery acid. Meth has many street names, including "speed," "Tina," "crystal," and "chalk."

The use of methamphetamine is extremely dangerous. Meth is one of the most addictive illegal substances, according to the National Institute on Drug Abuse (NIDA). Meth releases high levels of dopamine into the brain and acts as a mood enhancer, providing the user with a rush, with a false sense of ecstasy and control. This extra sense of pleasure is followed by a crash that impairs the user and leads to more craving. The immediate side effects can include convulsions, dangerous fevers, strokes, heart irregularities, stomach cramps, and shaking.

The long-term effects of using methamphetamine are even more devastating. The user builds up tolerance, so it takes more meth to get that rush. Users don't eat or sleep while they're looking for drugs, obsessed with trying to repeat that initial rush. After they don't sleep for days, they become exhausted, paranoid, and angry. Their teeth become rotten. They smell like chemicals, including cat urine. Many feels like bugs are crawling under their skin, and they scratch so hard that they develop ugly and infected open sores. Meth can also cause cardiovascular damage and brain damage.

The use of methamphetamine presents a danger to all users, but it presents an even greater danger to children. Meth use has risen in recent years among teens, who are often introduced to the drug at a party. Some users, particularly teenage girls, use the drug as a weight-loss aid. According to the DEA, one out of five people who enter treatment for meth addiction is

DEA agents making an arrest in California during Operation Wildfire, an attack on meth manufacturing and distribution networks.

under the age of 18. "Meth has spread like wildfire across the United States," Tandy said. "It has burned out communities, scorched childhoods, and charred once happy and productive lives beyond recognition."

The DEA has focused significant attention on methamphetamine. Cracking down on meth use is especially difficult because the drug is "homemade, cheap, and readily available," Tandy explained. In 2005 the DEA launched a sweep called Operation Wildfire, which was intended to strike all levels of meth manufacturing and distribution in the U.S. Coordinating with partners from state and local law enforcement agencies, the DEA arrested 400 people in 200 U.S. cities for producing and selling meth. The DEA also seized more than 200 pounds of meth and closed 56 labs that made it. Some of the labs were small operations, such as one found in a hotel room in Minneapolis. They also seized 28 vehicles and 123 weapons, and removed 30 children from dangerous environments.

"The consequences of meth are undeniable—for the abuser, for the trafficker, for the environment, for communities, and for the innocent children who live in filth and neglect," Tandy said. "Methamphetamine abuse has ruined families, destroyed neighborhoods, put a tremendous strain on all

153

levels of law enforcement and social services. This historic enforcement effort illustrates our commitment to extinguishing this plague and protecting innocent Americans from the harmful ripple effects meth leaves behind."

The War against Drugs Worldwide

As head of the DEA, Tandy's job is not limited to battling drug trafficking in the U.S. She is also responsible for the coordination of efforts by DEA agents with officials from other countries to combat international drug smuggling into the U.S. Less than three weeks after assuming the DEA leadership, Tandy traveled to Mexico for the first of many trips to try and strengthen international ties in the war against drugs. Tandy praised the joint U.S.-Mexican operation in July 2003 that led to the arrest of 240 drug-smuggling suspects on both sides of the border. Mexico and the U.S. "are committed to the same goals of ensuring that we protect national security in both countries from the evils of drug trafficking," she said.

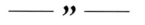

> "The consequences of meth are undeniable—for the abuser, for the trafficker, for the environment, for communities, and for the innocent children who live in filth and neglect," Tandy said. "Methamphetamine abuse has ruined families, destroyed neighborhoods, put a tremendous strain on all levels of law enforcement and social services."

But preventing drugs from other countries, including Mexico, from reaching the U.S. continues to be a serious problem. Government officials estimate that two-thirds of the methamphetamine that reaches the U.S. comes from Mexico. During Tandy's tenure as DEA Administrator, the agency also participated in antidrug operations in Canada, Colombia, the Dominican Republic, Panama, Jamaica, Afghanistan, and the Bahamas, among others. In one internationally coordinated sting in 2005, Operation Three Hour Tour, suspects were arrested in Colombia and the Dominican Republic the same day as their associates were arrested in California, New York, Connecticut, and Iowa. The arrests destroyed three major drug transportation rings that together smuggled the following into the United States each month: 4,000 pounds of cocaine, 20-30 pounds of heroin, and more than 50 pounds of meth. Thousands of pounds of illegal drugs and millions of dollars were seized, including 3,163 pounds of cocaine, 216 pounds of marijuana, 55

DEA agents and police officers ready to strike in Operation Mallorca,
an attack on money-laundering activities by Colombian drug lords
and U.S. criminal organizations.

pounds of meth, 15 pounds of heroin, 10,000 doses of ecstasy, $5.5 million in cash, 58 vehicles, and 52 firearms.

Since becoming the DEA administrator, Tandy has made use of her expertise in forfeiture law. She has focused on seizing drug merchants' assets, which have included airplanes, boats, houses, jewelry, and furs. "When I came through the door, I made money the No.1 priority," she said. In her first three years as administrator, the value of goods seized by the DEA more than quadrupled, to $1.9 billion annually.

One such operation was Operation Mallorca. This was a 27-month investigation into the money-laundering activities of several Columbian-based brokers who used drug proceeds to buy other goods. Money laundering means using a series of financial transactions to conceal the source or destination of funds—for example, taking drug money and moving it from one account to another, many times, so that the final placement of the funds can't be traced to the original drug money. The operation resulted in 36 arrests, including 13 traffickers who had handled $12 million in drug money and laundered it through 300 wire transfers to 200 bank accounts in 16 cities and 13 foreign countries. "DEA is targeting the financial networks of drug cartels like never before to bankrupt traffickers and money launderers," Tandy explained. "In Operation Mallorca, we followed the money around the globe and into the hands of three Colombia drug traffickers. . . . DEA showed today that traffickers can move their money around the world, but we will track it down."

The War against Internet Drug Crime

The DEA has also investigated drug crimes involving the Internet, both in the U.S. and overseas. In July 2004, in Operation Web Tryp, DEA agents arrested 10 people in five states and targeted 10 web sites that distributed drug analogues (copies of drugs that are designed to look real) to unsuspecting customers. Two young men, one 18 and the other 22, died after ingesting chemicals purchased from two of the sites. "The formulation of analogues is like a drug dealer's magic trick meant to fool law enforcement," Tandy said. "They didn't fool us and we must educate our children so they are not fooled either."

In 2005 the DEA created a new Virtual Enforcement Initiative to prevent drug criminals from using modern technology to spread drug use. The first drug sting was Operation Cyber Chase in April 2005. This investigation resulted in 20 arrests in eight U.S. cities and four foreign countries. This operation targeted major traffickers who sold narcotics, amphetamines, and anabolic steroids directly to buyers of all ages without a prescription from a doctor. "In this first major international enforcement action against on-line rogue pharmacies and their sources of supply," said Tandy, "we've logged these traffickers off the Internet."

Another 2005 sting targeting illegal Internet drugs, Operation Gear Grinder, was a 21-month investigation into eight major steroid manufacturing companies, as well as their owners. "Steroid traffickers market their product by luring young people with promises of enhanced performance and appearance," Tandy said, "but what they don't say is the illicit use of these harmful drugs can destroy the very bodies that they are supposed to improve. Drug traffickers prey on the belief that steroids enhance ability, but steroids only rob that ability, as we have seen so often from the affected lives of too many youth and professional athletes."

Creating a Web Site for Young People

A cornerstone of Tandy's work at the DEA has been her determination to steer young people away from drug use. "It is every parent's worst nightmare," she said. "I have two teenaged daughters and I'm no different than any other parent—I worry about my kids. They are great kids, but peer pressure can be a big issue."

Tandy decided that the best way to reach young people is through the Internet. In 2005 she authorized and helped develop www.justthinktwice.com, a web site designed to show teenagers the consequences of illegal-drug use. The site, which includes animation, colorful graphics, and videos of former drug users, has been praised by teenagers, school officials, and parents for its ease of use and wealth of information. The "DEA is providing primary source information to help teens make good decisions," said Tandy. "We're taking them directly to the data and objective sources of medical, scientific and legal information."

The web site is divided into several sections, each of which discusses the dangers of specific drugs, including cough syrup, marijuana, methamphetamine, heroin, and steroids. Clicking on the cough-syrup link, for example, pulls up an animated character that yawns, burps, and scratches his belly—all while pointing to a second link that asks: "What's the big deal about DMX (dextromethorphan) anyway?" The potential serious side effects of vomiting, cardiac arrest, muscle spasms, and delirium are shown in a cartoon with the same animated character.

—— " ——

Tandy is determined to steer young people away from drug use. "It is every parent's worst nightmare," she said. "I have two teenaged daughters and I'm no different than any other parent—I worry about my kids. They are great kids, but peer pressure can be a big issue."

—— " ——

Not all of the links are entertaining. The site features pictures of drug users' rotting teeth, for example, and the disturbing before and after pictures of methamphetamine users. There are also short videos of young people talking about their negative experiences with drugs, as well as a link for treatment options and counseling centers for people who need help. "There is no more powerful message for teens than hearing from their peers about the impact that drugs had on other young lives," said Tandy.

For young people who have questions about drugs that they are reluctant to ask adults, the web site features a "Teens Ask Teens" option. Six teenage volunteers from the Drug Abuse Resistance Education (DARE) Advisory

*Tandy announcing the successful results of an
Internet trafficking case, Operation Cyber Chase.*

Committee are profiled and are available to answer questions through an email link.

The justthinktwice web site also focuses on the dangers of ordering prescription drugs, particularly Vicodin and Xanax, from the Internet. Drug transactions without a prescription are illegal, and doing so can lead to fatal consequences, as it did for two teenagers whose stories are told on the site. "The Internet has become the street corner for many of the drug users and traffickers," Tandy said. "These dealers now enter the privacy of our homes to entice and sell destruction to our children veiled under the illusion of being safe and legal."

Stumbleweed

The justthinktwice web site also includes an on-line magazine, *Stumbleweed*, which highlights the potential dangers of using marijuana. Readers can click on four articles: "Hey Dude, Where Did My Future Go"; "Totally Lame (and Dangerous and Illegal) Things to Do on Pot"; "Rx Pot: A Prescription for Disaster"; and "It's Just a Plant: How Could It Be Bad for Me?" Like the rest of the DEA site, *Stumbleweed* uses appealing graphics and cartoons in addition to providing a lot of informational text and a strong anti-drug message.

Tandy's strong stand against marijuana, even for medical uses, has been criticized by advocates who favor decriminalizing the substance. But Tandy has said that her concern about children is an important reason for her hard line. "We have more teens in (counseling) for marijuana than for all other drugs combined, including alcohol," she said.

> "[The] DEA is reminding kids to 'just think twice' about what they hear about marijuana from their friends, popular culture, and adults," Tandy said. "Think about the harm drugs cause to families, the environment, to innocent bystanders. Think about how drugs will impact your future: your health, your chances for a good job, your eligibility for student loans."

Stumbleweed argues that marijuana is not just a harmless plant. It's the active chemical ingredient in marijuana, THC, that makes people high. Marijuana with more THC is more potent and more likely to cause short-term memory loss, poor judgment, and impaired driving ability. "[The] DEA is reminding kids to 'just think twice' about what they hear about marijuana from their friends, popular culture, and adults," Tandy said. "Think about the harm drugs cause to families, the environment, to innocent bystanders. Think about how drugs will impact your future: your health, your chances for a good job, your eligibility for student loans."

In addition to its efforts in the area of education, the DEA sponsors programs for teenagers who are interested in a career in law enforcement and participating in drug prevention activities. One such program, the Law Enforcement Explorers, has posts across the country, and focuses on career development, leadership, citizenship and life skills. Another program, Teens in Prevention (TIP), focuses on mobilizing positive peer interactions and community support to reduce drug abuse and violence. More information on both programs is available on the justthinktwice web site.

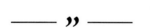

"It just doesn't get any better than this—leading 11,000 extraordinarily gifted people in DEA around the world who sacrifice everything to live our dangerous mission 24-7, every day of the year, in order to protect America's children and communities."

Leaving the DEA

Tandy racked up some impressive accomplishments during her tenure at the DEA. As DEA administrator, she directed investigations that resulted in criminal charges against 87 percent of the most wanted drug trafficking leaders. She aggressively seized drug proceeds and assets, with $3.75 billion in seized drug assets from 2004 to 2006. She led DEA initiatives to wipe out meth labs. She worked to strengthen the DEA's partnerships around the world. She met with heads of state from many different countries and initiated intelligence-sharing agreements with China and Russia. She deployed teams of DEA agents to conduct operations in Afghanistan against Taliban-connected drug lords, resulting in the seizure of opium, heroin, and drug labs.

By late 2007, Tandy was ready for a change. After more than 30 years of public service, she announced she was retiring from the DEA. "It just doesn't get any better than this—leading 11,000 extraordinarily gifted people in DEA around the world who sacrifice everything to live our dangerous mission 24-7, every day of the year, in order to protect America's children and communities," she said. "I will forever remain grateful to President Bush for this opportunity."

In October 2007, Tandy joined Motorola as the Senior Vice President of the Global Government Relations and Public Policy Division. In this position, she will be the company's top spokesperson on issues related to global telecom policy, trade, regulation, and related matters. She will be working on policy issues both within the United States and around the world. Gene Delaney, a Motorola executive, was enthusiastic about her role with the company. "Karen's substantial international relations and government affairs experience, as well as her policy understanding, make her an ideal and logical fit to lead our government and policy team," Delaney said. "We are confident that she will play an integral role in Motorola's continued success both in North America and around the world."

MARRIAGE AND FAMILY

Tandy lives in Virginia with her husband, Steven Pomerantz, a retired FBI agent, and their two daughters, Lauren and Kimberly. In her spare time, she serves as a Girl Scout leader and helps organize food drives for homeless children.

HONORS AND AWARDS

Attorney General's Award for Distinguished Service
Department of Justice Award for Extraordinary Achievement
United States Attorney Director's Award for Superior Service
Women in Federal Law Enforcement Director's Award: 2004
Texas Tech University School of Law Distinguished Alumna Award: 2004
Public Service Award from the Drug Abuse Resistance Education (DARE): 2005

FURTHER READING

Books

Who's Who in America, 2007

Periodicals

Fort Worth Star Telegram, June 26, 2003, p.A1; July 11, 2004, p.A5
Houston Chronicle, Aug. 2, 2003, p.A8; Sept. 28, 2003, pp.A1 and A33; May 21, 2006, p.A12
New York Times, Aug. 31, 2005, p.A16
Washington Post, Aug. 31, 2005, p.A2

Online Databases

Biography Resource Center Online, 2007, article from *Carroll's Federal Directory,* 2007

ADDRESS

Karen P. Tandy
Motorola Inc.
1301 East Algonquin Road
Schaumberg, IL 60196

WORLD WIDE WEB SITES

http://www.usdoj.gov/dea/index.htm
http://www.justthinktwice.com
http://www.motorola.com

Photo and Illustration Credits

Front Cover Photos: Hudgens: Jennifer Graylock/Associated Press; Niedermayer: Jim McIsaac/Getty Images; Oka: Paul Drinkwater/NBC Photo. Copyright © 2007 NBC Universal, Inc. All Rights Reserved.; Rowling: Eamonn McCormack/WireImage.com.

Greta Binford/Photos: Courtesy Lewis & Clark College (pp. 9, 15 center, bottom); Jim Kalisch/University of Nebraska Department of Entomology (p. 15 top); Courtesy Greta Binford/Lewis & Clark College (pp. 17, 19).

Cory Booker/Photos: Courtesy Mayor's Office, Newark, New Jersey (pp. 23, 34); Tim Davis/Stanford Athletics (p. 26); DVD: STREET FIGHT © 2005 Marshall Curry Productions, LLC. Package design © Genius Products, LLC. All Rights Reserved. Photographs © The Star Ledger, Newark, NJ. (p. 30).

Vanessa Hudgens/Photos: Jesse Grant/WireImage/Getty (p. 37); DVD cover: HIGH SCHOOL MUSICAL: ENCORE EDITION copyright © Disney. All Rights Reserved. (p. 41); CD: VANESSA HUDGENS V © ℗ 2006 Hollywood Records, Inc. All Rights Reserved. Photo by Andrew MacPherson. Art direction and design by Enny Joo. Creative director: David Snow. (p. 43); Copyright © Disney. All Rights Reserved. (p. 45).

Jennifer Hudson/Photos: Marcel Thomas/FilmMagic/Getty (p. 49); AMERICAN IDOL. Logo. ™©2006 FOX BROADCASTING CR:FOX (p. 52); Ray Mickshaw/WireImage/Getty (p. 53); Frank Micelotta/Getty Images (p. 55); David James/copyright © 2006 Dreamworks LLC and Paramount Pictures. All Rights Reserved. (p. 57); Gary Hershorn/Reuters/Landov (p. 60).

Zach Hunter/Photos: Photo by Tom Sapp/courtesy Penny Hunter (p. 63); Ted Haddock/International Justice Mission® (p. 66, 68); BE THE CHANGE: YOUR GUIDE TO FREEING SLAVES AND CHANGING THE WORLD (Zondervan Publishing) Copyright © 2007 by Zach Hunter. Cover Photography: The Visual Reserve. Cover Design: Burnkit. Creative Team: Doug Davidson, Rich Cairnes, Heather Haggerty, and David Conn. (p. 71).

Jonas Brothers/Photos: Kevin Parry/WireImage/Getty (p. 73); Frank Micelotta/Getty Images for Fox (p. 76); CD: JONAS BROTHERS © ℗ 2007 Hollywood Records. All Rights Reserved. (p. 79); Mathew Imaging/FilmMagic/Getty (p. 81).

Scott Niedermayer/Photos: Mike Cassese/Reuters/Landov (p. 85); Scott Levy/Getty Images (p. 87); Brian Clarkson/Associated Press (p. 90); Jeff Vinnick/Stringer/Getty Images (p. 92); Jim McIsaac/Getty Images (p. 95).

Masi Oka/Photos: Chris Haston/NBC Photo. Copyright © 2007 NBC Universal, Inc. All Rights Reserved. (p. 99); DVD: THE PERFECT STORM copyright © 2000 Warner

Cumulative Names Index

This cumulative index includes the names of all individuals profiled in *Biography Today* since the debut of the series in 1992.

Aaliyah . . . . Jan 02
Aaron, Hank. . . . . Sport V.1
Abbey, Edward . . . . WorLdr V.1
Abdul, Paula . . . . Jan 92; Update 02
Abdul-Jabbar, Kareem. . . . . Sport V.1
Abzug, Bella . . . . Sep 98
Adams, Ansel. . . . . Artist V.1
Adams, William (will.i.am)
   see Black Eyed Peas . . . . Apr 06
Adams, Yolanda. . . . . Apr 03
Adu, Freddy . . . . Sport V.12
Affleck, Ben . . . . Sep 99
Agassi, Andre . . . . Jul 92
Agosto, Ben . . . . Sport V.14
Aguilera, Christina . . . . Apr 00
Aidid, Mohammed Farah . . . . . WorLdr V.2
Aikman, Troy . . . . Apr 95; Update 01
Alba, Jessica . . . . Sep 01
Albright, Madeleine . . . . Apr 97
Alcindor, Lew
   see Abdul-Jabbar, Kareem. . . . . . Sport V.1
Aldrich, George . . . . Science V.11
Alexander, Lloyd . . . . Author V.6
Ali, Laila . . . . Sport V.11
Ali, Muhammad . . . . Sport V.2
Allen, Marcus . . . . Sep 97
Allen, Tim . . . . Apr 94; Update 99
Allen, Tori. Sport V.9
Alley, Kirstie. . . . . Jul 92
Almond, David. . . . . Author V.10
Alvarez, Julia. . . . . Author V.17
Alvarez, Luis W.. . . . . Science V.3
Amanpour, Christiane. . . . . Jan 01
Amend, Bill. . . . . Author V.18
Amin, Idi . . . . WorLdr V.2
Amman, Simon . . . . Sport V.8
An Na . . . . Author V.12
Anders, C.J.
   see Bennett, Cherie . . . . Author V.9

Anderson, Brett (Donna A.)
   see Donnas . . . . Apr 04
Anderson, Gillian. . . . . Jan 97
Anderson, Laurie Halse . . . . . . Author V.11
Anderson, Marian . . . . Jan 94
Anderson, Terry. . . . . Apr 92
André 3000
   see OutKast . . . . Sep 04
Andretti, Mario . . . . Sep 94
Andrews, Ned . . . . Sep 94
Angelou, Maya. . . . . Apr 93
Aniston, Jennifer. . . . . Apr 99
Annan, Kofi . . . . Jan 98; Update 01
Anthony, Carmelo. . . . . Sep 07
apl.de.ap (Alan Pineda Lindo)
   see Black Eyed Peas . . . . Apr 06
Applegate, K.A.. . . . . Jan 00
Arafat, Yasir . Sep 94; Update 94; Update 95;
   Update 96; Update 97; Update 98;
   Update 00; Update 01; Update 02
Arantes do Nascimento, Edson
   see Pelé . . . . Sport V.1
Aristide, Jean-Bertrand . . Jan 95; Update 01
Armstrong, Billie Joe
   see Green Day. . . . . Apr 06
Armstrong, Lance.. . . . . . Sep 00; Update 00;
   Update 01; Update 02
Armstrong, Robb . . . . Author V.9
Armstrong, William H.. . . . . Author V.7
Arnesen, Liv . . . . Author V.15
Arnold, Roseanne . . . . Oct 92
Asbaty, Diandra . . . . Sport V.14
Ashanti. . . . . PerfArt V.2
Ashe, Arthur . . . . Sep 93
Ashley, Maurice . . . . Sep 99
Asimov, Isaac . . . . Jul 92
Askins, Renee . . . . WorLdr V.1
Attenborough, David . . . . Science V.4
Atwater-Rhodes, Amelia . . . . . . Author V.8
Aung San Suu Kyi . . . . . Apr 96; Update 98;
   Update 01; Update 02

For cumulative general, places of birth, and birthday indexes, please see biographytoday.com.

165

For cumulative general, places of birth, and birthday indexes, please see biographytoday.com.

For cumulative general, places of birth, and birthday indexes, please see biographytoday.com.

171

For cumulative general, places of birth, and birthday indexes, please see biographytoday.com.

175

For cumulative general, places of birth, and birthday indexes, please see biographytoday.com.

For cumulative general, places of birth, and birthday indexes, please see biographytoday.com.

For cumulative general, places of birth, and birthday indexes, please see biographytoday.com.

179

Biography Today
General Series

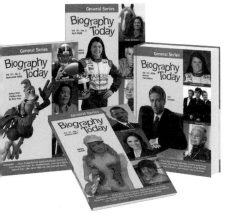

Biography Today **General Series** includes a unique combination of current biographical profiles that teachers and librarians — and the readers themselves — tell us are most appealing. The **General Series** is available as a 3-issue subscription; hardcover annual cumulation; or subscription plus cumulation.

Within the **General Series**, your readers will find a variety of sketches about:

- Authors
- Musicians
- Political leaders
- Sports figures
- Movie actresses & actors
- Cartoonists
- Scientists
- Astronauts
- TV personalities
- and the movers & shakers in many other fields!

Biography Today **will be useful in elementary and middle school libraries and in public library children's collections where there is a need for biographies of current personalities. High schools serving reluctant readers may also want to consider a subscription."**
— *Booklist*, American Library Association

Highly recommended for the young adult audience. Readers will delight in the accessible, energetic, tell-all style; teachers, librarians, and parents will welcome the clever format [and] intelligent and informative text. It should prove especially useful in motivating 'reluctant' readers or literate nonreaders."
— *MultiCultural Review*

Written in a friendly, almost chatty tone, the profiles offer quick, objective information. While coverage of current figures makes *Biography Today* a useful reference tool, an appealing format and wide scope make it a fun resource to browse." — *School Library Journal*

The best source for current information at a level kids can understand."
— Kelly Bryant, School Librarian, Carlton, OR

Easy for kids to read. We love it! Don't want to be without it."
— Lynn McWhirter, School Librarian, Rockford, IL

ONE-YEAR SUBSCRIPTION
- 3 softcover issues, 6" x 9"
- Published in January, April, and September
- 1-year subscription, list price $66. **School and library price $64**
- 150 pages per issue
- 10 profiles per issue
- Contact sources for additional information
- Cumulative Names Index

HARDBOUND ANNUAL CUMULATION
- Sturdy 6" x 9" hardbound volume
- Published in December
- List price $73. **School and library price $66 per volume**
- 450 pages per volume
- 30 profiles — includes all profiles found in softcover issues for that calendar year
- Cumulative General Index, Places of Birth Index, and Birthday Index

SUBSCRIPTION AND CUMULATION COMBINATION
- $110 for 3 softcover issues plus the hardbound volume

For Cumulative General, Places of Birth, and Birthday Indexes, please see www.biographytoday.com.